Long Island, the Global Economy, and Race

The Aging of America's First Suburb

Martin R. Cantor

LONG ISLAND, THE GLOBAL ECONOMY, AND RACE

THE AGING OF AMERICA'S FIRST SUBURB.

PRINTED IN THE UNITED STATES OF AMERICA

$16.00 U.S.

ISBN-13: 978-0-9789783-0-3
ISBN-10: 0-9789783-0-7

51600

9 780978 978303

This book is dedicated to the Long Islander's who built the suburb that
we all enjoy today and to,

Irwin Quintyne, Rosemarie Dearing, Lenny Canton,
Dee Thompson, and Andreaus 13,
whose personal experiences brought life to this book

and

thanks to Bradley Cantor, MS Urban Planning, for designing the cover
and for his research assistance.

Long Island, The Global Economy, and Race
The Aging of America's First Suburb

Table of Contents

Chapter I

PROLOGUE:
LONG ISLAND, AMERICA'S FIRST SUBURB:
LAYING THE FOUNDATION
FOR SOCIAL AND ECONOMIC INEQUALITY

Long Island New York, America's first suburb, has been part of the Nation's history from the very beginning. Whether it was religious freedom or free trade that brought the first settlers to New York and Long Island, the region has been an integral part of American history. From Long Island came: financial support for the War for Independence and the Culpepper Revolutionary War Spy Ring; President Theodore Roosevelt and his contribution to environmental causes, business reform, and the Spanish American War; the homes of the rich and famous on Long Island's Gold Coast; and Roosevelt Field, where Charles Lindberg departed for Europe on his historic flight, and which later became America's first indoor shopping Mall.

The annals of flight are replete with Long Island's contributions to aviation and America's defense through fighter plane construction at Fairchild-Republic and Grumman Aviation. It was also Long Islander's who responded to President John Kennedy's challenge to put an American on the moon by the end of the 1960's by designing and building the Lunar Module that took the first men to the Moon and safely back to Earth.

In the area of science and research, Long Island is home to Nobel Laureates in regional Universities, the Cold Spring Harbor Laboratory and the Brookhaven National Laboratory. No matter what the cause, Long Island has had strong influences on American science, exploration, defense and sociology.

Yet despite all these accomplishment, standing out as the most sociological significant was the post World War II housing boom that transformed 4,000 acres in a tranquil Nassau County potato farming community into Levittown, America's first suburb.

Now more than a half-century later, the population of contemporary Long Island has grown larger than 22 states, and is quite different from what it was when the men and women came back from World War II to settle in Levittown. While Levittown remains basically unchanged, present-day Long Island has grown beyond its rural roots and the primarily white population to become a multi-cultural region with a multi-faceted economy, which together with New York City drives much of the New York State economy.

Yet, not all Long Islander's had shared in the societal and economic growth of the 60 years since World War II ended; beginning with returning African-American war veterans who found that they would not be able to live in Levittown. They learned that while there were no restrictions about putting their life on the line in war, that wasn't considered important to those who did not want to be their neighbor.

One such returning veteran was Irwin Quintyne, who I met while a consultant for the town of Babylon. My assignment was to assist the local community group NACEC with their revitalization efforts for North Amityville. Quintyne was retired from the New York City garment industry, in his 70's, and still married to the woman he was introduced to in the 1960's when he passed away in 2004. Seeking a better quality of life, Quintyne moved to North Amityville in the early 1960's from the St. Nick housing projects in Harlem,

CHAPTER I

located on 131st Street between 7th and 8th avenues. What lured him to Long Island were memories he had as a youngster when his mother took him to visit friends in Queens, because the friend's home had grass, a back yard, and room to play. Irwin wanted his children to grow up in similar surroundings. He originally tried to buy a home in Levittown, but because he was black he experienced discrimination, and confronted home sellers not interested in selling him a home, despite the fact that he, and many of his fellow black veterans wished to settle in Levittown.[1]

Quintyne recalled that his friend lived in North Amityville, where, during his younger days he would watch the New York Giants away football games. He inquired about homes and found that many black World War II veterans, unable to buy homes in Levittown, had settled in North Amityville. Quintyne, while reading the *Amsterdam News*, a Harlem newspaper, found an advertisement for a house in North Amityville. He saw the house and bought it, financed with a GI loan. However, because the house had serious design flaws, leading to continuous flooding, he moved to a neighboring community, eventually returning to North Amityville where he lived until his death in 2004.[2]

Another example is Rosemarie Dearing, a graduate of West Virginia State University, who moved to North Amityville from Virginia in 1963 to live with her sister, who was married to Irwin Quintyne. At that time Dearing had just left her husband, and with her two-year-old son came north. She has remained single, and was employed in the biology departments of Brookhaven National Laboratory and Amityville based Brunswick Hospital. Her son has graduated from Morgan State College.[3]

Dearing recalls that North Amityville in the early 1960's was a friendly and close-knit community where everyone knew everyone else. The community was one where doors were left open and unlocked. Dearing recalled going to sleep one summer night forgetting to lock the screen door, yet awakening the next day to find that all was secure, contrary to today when doors are securely locked.[4]

Things, however, began to change in the late 1960's and early 1970's, a time punctuated by the racial unrest in American cities and communities. While there were no riots in North Amityville, there was nonetheless, a developing sense of tenseness and turmoil, centered on demonstrations, sit-ins, protests against patterns of discrimination in job hiring, and a growing distrust of the police.

In this atmosphere, during the late 1960's, Dearing moved to a Copiague apartment, where one side of the street was in Copiague and the other side in North Amityville. She lived there for two years and then moved back to North Amityville to a nicer apartment near the middle school. She shared a home with four friends in a neighborhood that was relatively peaceful. However all this was about to change. During the 1970's drugs began to proliferate, especially among the younger children. House robberies increased causing people to lock their doors, relegating many to remain behind those doors for fear of robbery.[5]

In the early 1980's the drug trade intensified, leading not only to an increase in crime, but crime that became more violent with guns more noticeable. Dearing wanted to leave North Amityville, but decided that she wasn't going to let crime drive her out of town.[6]

[1] Irwin Quintyne. Personal Interview. 18 May 2001.
[2] Ibid.
[3] Rosemarie Dearing. Personal Interview. 18 May 2001. Personal Interview updated 27 August 2006.
[4] Ibid.
[5] Ibid.
[6] Ibid.

Schools at that time had not yet become a problem for Dearing, because her son went to the primarily white Copiague schools, was doing well and from where he ultimately graduated. The relative calm was shattered during the 1970's when a racist group developed in the Copiague schools and tried to get the blacks out of the schools. Dearing recalled that blacks knew where not to go. For instance, nearby Lindenhurst was known to be off limits to blacks while Copiague was partially off limits. Discrimination reached its high point when a march was organized on the Copiague school intended to tell blacks what would happen to them if they didn't leave Copiague. While a larger counter demonstration was held against the racist march, an atmosphere of racism remained.[7]

Another long time North Amityville resident is Lenny Canton, an accountant now practicing in North Amityville. Canton, originally from 117th Street between 5th and Lenox Avenues in Harlem moved to North Amityville in the 1950's. Canton recalls that his mother, believing that New York City was changing in its attitudes towards blacks, didn't want him to grow up in an apartment near the New York City housing projects that were under construction. Thus, Canton moved to a single-family house in North Amityville with his two brothers, his mother and his father. One brother earned a Master's degree and is now a retired teacher, while the other holds a Ph.D. in Education Administration and is currently teaching at the University of Sacramento. Of Canton's two children, both educated in the Copiague school system, and both attended college. One graduated college, and worked for Chase Bank until her job was outsourced to Canada. She currently is an auditor for the New York State Comptroller. The other was unable to finish college because she became afflicted with Muscular Sclerosis. However she now has become an author and has published two books. Her latest and her third is a guide to full figured brides.[8]

Canton recalls that things were great in the 1960's. The worst of the urban problems of many metropolitan areas, such as discrimination, had yet to reach North Amityville. But in the 1970's things began to get worse. Families that had originally come to North Amityville to escape New York City moved away, and as the drug problems and criminal activity increased between 1975 and 1980, a transient population of those losing their jobs and those not being able to find ones replaced the once stable homeowners. Many of these new homeowners did not care about their homes or neighborhood, leading to the deterioration of the North Amityville community. By 1983, as the real influx of drugs took hold, everything went to seed.[9]

Whereas in the early 1970's, neighborhood security was taken for granted, residents could safely walk around, and businesses flourished; by the late 1970's and mid 1980's, the rash of burglaries and proliferation of the drug trade had replaced the sense of serenity and security with fear of violent crime, with businesses folding and people unable to sell their homes.[10]

Compounding the social impact from the drug trafficking and violent crime on the North Amityville community was the loss of economic activity caused by the contraction of the local employed workforce. Many young people dependent on the defense industry for jobs were left unemployed due to the closing of Fairchild-Republic and the downsizing of Grumman Corp. Canton's father worked for Fairchild-Republic, and when he was laid off it was financially catastrophic to the family. To save the family home, Canton's

[7] Ibid.
[8] Lenny Canton. Personal Interview. 18 May 2001. Personal Interview updated 27 August 2006.
[9] Ibid.
[10] Ibid.

father worked as a general tradesman doing painting and wallpapering. Others were not so fortunate, with many in North Amityville losing their homes; especially noteworthy since monthly mortgage payments for many was only $70. Of others who could afford the mortgages, some decided to move out when their families became to big for the homes, turning their back on the neighborhood. Of the 11 original families that lived on Canton's block when he moved to North Amityville, only 2 families remain.[11]

The personal reflections of Quintyne, Dearing, and Canton were of a mid 1960 North Amityville community where there was little crime and a good quality of life. Residents felt very comfortable and secure, that is until the drug culture began to infiltrate the community, slowly at first, then growing rapidly. Crime increases followed, with robberies, home break-ins and shootings spreading throughout the community, so much so that the Federal Bureau of Investigation had now ranked the once peaceful neighborhood of North Amityville as the seventh most notorious drug locale in the United States.[12] People, fearing for crime and for their individual safety, no longer shopped in the community, which led to the deterioration of neighborhood businesses.[13]

To differing degrees, what was occurring in North Amityville was also happening in other segregated Long Island communities that were confronting the dual challenge of erosion of their social fabric and local economies. Each was dealing with the impact from the regional stagnation of the construction industry, the mid to late 1980's contraction of Long Island's prime defense contractors, and the closing of the Pilgrim State Psychiatric Hospital in the early 1990's. Many Long Islanders who worked as engineers in regional defense prime contractors such as Sperry, Grumman, Fairchild-Republic, and Eaton lost their jobs and left Long Island never to return. Others, less skilled, lost employment at Pilgrim State. As the ripple effect of these lost jobs percolated through the Long Island economy, those who lost their jobs did not find it easy to get new ones, while others lacking the skills heavily influenced by the requirements of the global economy were unable to access the jobs being created in the regional economy.

Many moved from their communities, while those who were untrained for jobs now required of the global economy were left economically behind. Irwin Quintyne's friends went to Virginia and to the West Coast to find work.[14]

Public education was also showing the strain of adapting to the demands of the global economy. As recalled by Quintyne, Dearing, and Canton, in the late 1960's, when the schools had more white children attending they were better. When local schools had become primarily black the education had grown progressively worse. One reason offered is that North Amityville, originally a larger multi-racial school district, had been broken into three districts, Copiague, Farmingdale and North Amityville, with blacks concentrated into North Amityville. After the district breakup, educational achievement of the students in North Amityville began to deteriorate.

Another factor too important to ignore is the racism prevalent in the post World War II era that relegated returning veterans and their families to communities where inequitable property tax systems would continuously underfund school systems responsible for educating and influencing generations of blue-collar and service sector workers. Yet despite these inequities, Long Islander's were able to sustain family budgets from blue-collar jobs

---

[11] Ibid.
[12] Lt. Edward Riley. "Weed and Seed" police commander, First Precinct, Suffolk County, Town of Babylon. Personal Interview. 16 November 1998.
[13] Irwin Quintyne. Personal Interview. 18 May 2001.
[14] Ibid.

found in the region's many machine shops that supported Long Island prime military contractors including Fairchild-Republic, Hazeltine Corporation, and the Grumman Corporation.

As Long Island continued to grow, several external global economic pressures began to impact Long Island's employment base, and the wages earned by the region's blue-collar workforce. The first was the contraction and deindustrialization of the regional defense industry brought about by the end of the cold war. The second was the advancing technology that made commerce between nations more efficient and now required job skills that were quite different from with skills required of earlier workforces. As compared to the well paying tool and dye and blue-collar economy of the post-World War II era, today's global economy is fundamentally based on technology and computers, requiring a workforce possessing greater intellectual skills and capabilities. These new jobs pay higher wages and require employees to have a higher level of educational attainment, which data reflects that many Long Island black households did not have.

The racism of the post World War II era, which impacted where black families could live and where their children would learn, was taking its toll on household income. The lower educational attainment in minority communities negatively impacted family income, resulting in a community economic base that was unable to provide adequate tax revenues necessary to fund minority school districts. Not surprisingly, reading and mathematic test scores fell. Thus began a trend of underfunded and underperforming school districts, that while improving continue to the present day.

The lower levels of educational attainment in economic lagging communities worked counter to what was needed to access the higher paying jobs being created in the regional economy. Ultimately, this continued the trend of lower household incomes in Long Island's minority communities.

What follows is a reflection of how Long Island, America's first suburb fared with; the changes demanded by an evolving global economy; the deindustrializaton and contraction of Long Island's machine shops and defense prime contractors; and beginning with the 1970's, a consuming reliance on computers and technology which transformed global commerce to an economic system based on real time transactions.

These factors, in particular, impacted Long Island's many machine shops, leading to workforce reductions that impacted much of the regions less skilled and less educated workers. At the same time, demand for more skilled and more educated workers was growing in Long Island's emerging high technology industries, as well as in the growing financial and banking sector resulting largely from the globalization of economic activity between 1970 and 1990.

Based on the personal reflections of Quintyne, Dearing, and Canton, it was natural to be drawn to how North Amityville, a primarily African-American community, fared during the early days of the global economy between 1970 and 1990 as compared to the surrounding Suffolk County. With Long Island's distribution of housing patterns influenced by race, it is natural to ask how other communities such as Port Washington, a primarily white Nassau County community; Roosevelt, a primarily African American Nassau County Community; and Huntington Station, a Suffolk County community of color fared during the maturing years of the global economy between 1990 and 2000 as compared to their surrounding county. Would these communities fare any different than North Amityville?

CHAPTER I

What would be the impact of this period of industrial and economic restructuring on the Long Island workforce and related economy? What would be the cost to the respective community of the loss of jobs requiring a lower level of education, such as blue-collar manufacturing and clerical that resulted from globalization? Would the residents be able to achieve the education and skills necessary for employment in the emerging and higher paying technology jobs, such as specialized financial services, and computer and telecommunication technology and their related commercial applications? Would the global economy and changes in technology, now requiring more intellectual skills,[15] impact the correlation between education and family income as compared to past years?

Most important is the evaluation of the sociological distribution of the jobs created by global economy and the resulting impact on the Long Island economy. Would the restructuring of the economic order in the global economy allow for sustainable job creation and economic development on Long Island? Former President Clinton's Council on Sustainable Development defined sustainable as "a growing economy that provides equitable opportunities for satisfying livelihoods and a safe, healthy, high quality of life for current and future generations."[16] The Council concluded that,"manufacturing will continue to be a critical part of the U.S. economy into the foreseeable future." They were also right when they concluded that the "focus on manufacturing is critical since the jobs created or lost in this sector will have the greatest impact on economies, whether they be at the national, state or local levels."

This is especially true for Long Island, where the manufacturing sector and the strength of its aerospace and defense industries were critical in weathering the recessions of the 1980s. When the region lost Fairchild-Republic followed by the Grumman Corporation and Hazeltine Corp., the ripple effect cost the manufacturing sector nearly 66,000 jobs. This significant job loss in such a vital sector prevented Long Island from escaping the effects of the recession of the early 1990s. The result was that Long Island took longer than most regions of the country to recover from the recession. The consequence was an abundance of vacant factory buildings, dislocated workers and a restructuring of the Long Island job base.

Manufacturing jobs, which once comprised 15.4 percent of the Long Island job base, had decreased from a 1987 level of 176,300 jobs to the 2000 level of 109,800 or 10 percent of the job base. By August 2005 the 87,900 manufacturing jobs now represented only 7 percent of the total employed Long Islanders. The 2006 job base is primarily service and wholesale/retail jobs; with the significant job loss in the manufacturing sector being replaced by these lower paying jobs. Since 1987, service sector jobs have grown in the Long Island economy, and now represent nearly 36 percent of the job base, a significant increase from the 25 percent in 1987. Unfortunately, it is doubtful that Long Island will ever recover its lost manufacturing jobs. The result is that Long Island has become a consumer driven economy that is very vulnerable to interest rate fluctuations and the consumers ability to borrow and spend. One need only to look at how consumers and home-buyers were impacted by the rate increases of the Federal Reserve Board over the past several years. The combination of interest rate increases and wage growth stagnation has resulted in the current shortfall of regional sales tax revenues and depressed regional resi-

[15] William Julius Wilson, *When Work Disappears, The World of the New Urban Poor* (New York: Alfred A. Knopf,1997), p. 152.
[16] *Sustainable America - A New Consensus for Prosperity, Opportunity and a Healthy Environment for the Future.* Washington, D.C., February 1996.

dential home sales. An economy vulnerable to recession has now replaced the solid and sustainable economic manufacturing and construction industry foundation that once had insulated Long Island's economy from prior recessions.

President Clinton's Council on Sustainability concluded that resources "aspire to produce, use, and export globally competitive goods and services that use resources efficiently and result in fewer adverse side effects on natural systems and human health." The uniqueness of sustainability is its adaptability, and therein lies the future for Long Island. The export of goods and services, while importing dollars and economic activity is as relevant to the economy of Long Island and its communities as it is for the nation.

However the question that lingers for a sustainable Long Island is whether it is true that people of color tend to live in poorer communities with underfunded educational systems, have overstressed family support structures, and have lagged behind whites in educational attainment, employment, and household income. Or whether a system of institutional racism, whether covert or overt, intentional or not, has placed people of color in that circumstance.

The fact is that for whatever the reason, in the new Global Economy, the result is that in these Long Island communities, the income gap has widened between the haves and have-nots, and has usually fallen along racial lines. It is natural therefore, to ask what the impact would be on the communities-of-color of North Amityville, Roosevelt and Huntington Station, as compared to their respective home county of Nassau or Suffolk and to the predominately white community of greater Port Washington?

Driving the regional economic changes are the technological workforce demanded by the global economy, and the requirement of higher educational attainment for employment in higher paying jobs. How these demands have impacted the socio-economic fabric of Long Island and North Amityville, Huntington Station, Roosevelt, and Port Washington, good or bad, leads us through this discussion of how the global economy and race have influenced the aging of Long Island, America's First Suburb.

CHAPTER I

Chapter II

WORKFORCE IMPACT:
GLOBALIZATION AND CHANGING
TECHNOLOGY

The global economy is based on changes in technology and communications, whereby capital flows, commodity markets, information, raw materials, management and organization have become internationalized and fully interdependent.

The evolution of our industrial system, between 1970 and 1990, brought with it an economy emphasizing services and finances and a renewed focus to major cities for specific production, services, marketing and innovation. Furthermore, the internationalization of mergers, acquisitions, and financial transactions made cities the ideal center for management and coordination, for the raising and consolidations of investment capital, and for the formation of an international property market. This demand for financial innovations and specialized financial services continued, even during the period when major developments in computer and telecommunications technology and their related commercial applications occurred. What occurred was a change in the composition and growth patterns of the economies of major cities, now weighted heavily toward finance and producer services resulting from the above-average growth of these industrial sectors during the 1980's.[17] During this period of globalization, New York City increased its importance as a center of finance and as a center for global servicing and management. The New York City employment base lost 30 percent of its construction jobs, 22 percent of the manufacturing jobs and 20 percent of the transportation jobs. At the same time jobs in the wholesale/retail sector grew by 15 percent, by 21 percent in finance, insurance, and real estate, and respectively by 23, 42 and 62 percent in banking, and business and legal services sectors. Not only did these services sectors report an increase of jobs but their share of the New York City employment base also increased.[18] Long Island has fared no better, reporting similar changes to its employment base.

This new structure of global economic activity has brought changes in the organization of work, resulting in a shift in the job supply, and causing a polarization of the income and occupational distribution of workers. The growth industries of the global economy show a greater incidence of jobs at the high and low paying ends of the pay scale than do the jobs in the older industries now in decline. Almost half the jobs in the producer services are lower-wage jobs and half are in the two highest earnings class, in contrast to a large share of manufacturing workers who were in the middle-wage earning jobs during the postwar era. This economic polarization was caused, in part, by the downgrading of the manufacturing sector and the increase in the supply of low-wage jobs, reflected by the decline in the share of unionized shops and the deterioration of wages, while sweatshops and industrial homework proliferated. Additionally, the supply of low-wage jobs in restaurants, hotels, cleaners, luxury housing boutiques, etc., increased as required to service the new high-wage jobholders created by globalization. Important not to be lost is that the growth of jobs in the global economy brings not only higher wage technological jobs but

---

[17] Saskia Sassen, *The Global City: New York, London, Tokyo* (Princeton: Princeton University Press, 1991), p. 87-88.
[18] Ibid, p. 126-134.

also many low-paying jobs.[19] What prevents universal access to the higher paying jobs generated by the global economy, is that in the United States, only college graduates and those few with extra-specialized post-high school training have acquired the skills relevant to the demands of this highly technological marketplace. This differs from Japan and Germany, where most high school and college graduates leave school with the skills required for the global economy.[20]

Technological advances, now favoring intellectual over physical attributes of workers, have transferred skills once provided by workers to machines. Computers, with their attendant technical and professional personnel, have replaced blue-collar manufacturing jobs that were once epitomized by the assembly line. Further change is evident in what can be called the global assembly line, where production and assembly of goods originate from factories and depots throughout the world wherever labor costs and economies of scale make an international division of labor cost-effective. The globalization of production and assembly has created the need for increased centralization and complexity of management, control, and planning. The complexity of participating in world markets and foreign countries has resulted in diversification of product lines, mergers, and transnationalization of economic activities that require highly specialized skills in top-level management. This has fostered growth and development of higher levels of expertise among producer service firms such as accountants, attorneys, programmers, and financial, banking, public relations and management consultants, now being asked to improve upon their support services to where they now become crucial elements in corporate decision making. Thus, the multinational company, with its dispersed manufacturing facilities, contributes to the development of new types of planning in production and distribution required for its business.[21] While geographically Long Island, and in particular North Amityville, Huntington Station, Roosevelt, and Port Washington, may all be considered to be on the perimeter of the centers of global activity, the proximity to New York City, considered a leading global city, has impacted the Long Island region. The growth of Long Island's finance and banking sectors as well as the presence of many multi-national companies has brought the impact of the global economy to the region.

At the same time that changes in technology were producing new jobs; they were also making others obsolete. The technologically revolutionized workplace was widening the gap between skilled and unskilled workers, primarily because education and training had grown to become more important then ever. An example of this disparity is that in 1987 the average unadjusted annual pay in New York City was $28,735, as compared to $43,964 in the finance, insurance and real estate sector.[22]

Because of low levels of education, unskilled workers tend to be out of work or poorly paid, with others facing the threat of job displacement. For example, jobs created to develop new computer operated machine tools also eliminated jobs for those trained only for manual assembly-line work, and advances in word processing increased the demand for those who not only can type but who also can operate specialized software, often elim-

---

[19] Ibid. p. 9-10
[20] William Julius Wilson, *When Work Disappears, The World of the New Urban Poor* (New York:Alfred A Knopf, 1997), p. 221.
[21] Saskia Sassen, *The Global City: New York, London, Tokyo* (Princeton: Princeton University Press, 1991).
[22] Ibid, p. 224.

inating routine typists and secretaries.[23] This disappearance of work, caused by the structural changes of the global economy, subsequently impacting the distribution of jobs and the level of education required to obtain employment, resulted in the simultaneous occurrence of increasing joblessness and declining real wages for low-skilled workers. The decline of the mass production system, the decreasing availability of lower-skilled blue-collar jobs, and the growing importance of training and education in the higher-growth industries adversely affected the employment rates and earnings of low-skilled black workers.[24] The skills still taught in the public schools in the United States were principally designed to provide low-income native and immigrant students with the basic literacy and numeracy skills required for routine work in mass production factories, service industries, or farms. The interaction between technological and international competition demanded by the global economy has eroded the basic institutions of the mass production system, which has now become reliant on productivity improvements where human capital costs have been replaced by technology and the few educated professional, technical, and managerial workers necessary for production.[25] These relationships, in particular those of income and education, are presented in the following discussion.

EDUCATIONAL ATTAINMENT AND INCOME QUINTILES

The relationship between education and training and income distribution is complex, in as education's effect on income distribution is dependent not only on the way education is planned, developed and financed, but is also contingent upon such socioeconomic factors as employment probabilities, educational composition of the labor force, wage structure, and economic base. However, education does create a more skilled labor force which results in a shift from lower paid unskilled employment, to higher paid skilled employment. This shift produces higher labor incomes, a reduction in skill differentials, and an increase in the share of wages in total output. The increase in the number of more educated and skilled people will increase the ratio of such people in the total labor force while decreasing the ratio of less educated people.[26]

According to the World Bank, schooling, after controlling for the rate of economic growth, contributes significantly to a more equal income distribution in developing countries. As levels of schooling of the labor force increase, the income shares of both the bottom 40 percent and middle 40 percent of the population rise. Also important is that as the labor force gets more educated, income is redistributed from the top income quintile to the bottom 80 percent of the population.[27] Table 1 expresses the relationship between money income levels and educational attainment for families in the United States. New York State Department of Labor data indicates that there are higher paying jobs being created in the Long Island economy that require a higher degree of education, and by attaining that level of education a worker may be able to earn that higher paying job.

---

23 William Julius Wilson, *When Work Disappears, The World of the New Urban Poor* (New York: Alfred A. Knopf,1997), p. 152.
24 ibid, p. 54.
25 ibid, p. 151.
26 Jandhyala B.G. Tilak, *Education and Its Relation to Economic Growth, Poverty, and Income Distribution* (Washington:The World Bank, May 1980), p. 29-32.
27 Ibid, p. 77.

CHAPTER II
Table 1: Relationship Between 1998 Family Income Level and Educational Attainment
Income Levels ($1,000's)

Families	Total	Under $10,000	$10,000 to $14,999	$15,000 to $24,999	$25,000 to $34,999	$35,000 to $49,999	$50,000 to $74,999	$75,000 and Over
Total	71,551	4,593	3,799	8,811	9,052	11,995	15,427	17,874
With Education	68,309	3,846	3,427	8,088	8,562	11,539	15,111	17,736
% of Total	95%	84%	90%	92%	95%	96%	98%	99%
Below 9th Grade	7%	17%	20%	14%	9%	5%	2%	1%
9th-12th No Grad	9%	23%	19%	17%	12%	10%	5%	2%
High Sch grad	32%	34%	35%	37%	41%	37%	34%	19%
Some College	18%	15%	15%	17%	19%	21%	21%	16%
Assoc. Degree	8%	4%	5%	6%	7%	9%	10%	9%
College Grad.	17%	5%	4%	7%	9%	13%	20%	31%
Post Grad Deg	9%	2%	2%	2%	3%	5%	8%	22%

Source: U.S. Census Bureau, Statistical Abstract of The United States: 2000: Table 746. Money Income of Families-Distribution by Family Characteristics and Income level: 1998

Other research has shown that income is closely related to the level of education, as is the widening income gap. Robert Reich, in *The Works of Nations*, points out that a male with a high school diploma but no college education who is employed and earning $27,733 in 1987, will find that fourteen years earlier in 1973, someone with the same education would have earned $31,677, as expressed in 1987 dollars. Thus, with no more than a high school education, real earnings actually declined by 12 percent. That same male, if he had dropped out of high school and was working in 1987 would have earned $16,094, as compared to the $19,562 (expressed in 1987 dollars) he would have earned in 1973, a decline of 18 percent. For a graduate from a four-year college the earnings comparison would be different. The 1987 earnings of $50,115 would be comparable to the $49,531 (expressed in 1987 dollars) earned by a four-year college graduate in 1973. While a college degree does not guarantee that one will earn more, without it the chances are very slim that one will.[28]

The widening gap between rich and poor appears to be related to a growing divergence in how much money people receive for the work that they do, and that divergence appears to have something to do with education. As suggested by Table 1, if one graduated from college, earnings improved, if one did not, one tended to get poorer. Basic causes include, deindustrialization, technology replacing what manual labor once provided, and the global economy.[29] How these factors impacted various Long Island communities between 1970 and 2000 will be evaluated, beginning with North Amityville, and followed by Huntington Station, Roosevelt, and Port Washington.

[28] Robert B. Reich, *The Works of Nations* (New York: Vintage Books, 1992), p. 205-206
[29] ibid, p. 207.

Chapter III

NORTH AMITYVILLE:
OVERCOMING ECONOMIC STAGNATION

The 20 years between 1970 and 1990 brought socioeconomic changes to the New York City metropolitan area, including the primarily African-American community of North Amityville. Indeed, North Amityville has become more segregated. Several indices point to North Amityville's stagnation; as compared to the economic development that has characterized Suffolk County. There has been a significant drop in married households, and single headed households have increased dramatically to where they represent 3 in 8 families, more than double the rate of Suffolk County. The educational enrollment in advanced grades and overall educational attainment levels are much lower than in Suffolk County, and in part explain the bare increase in North Amityville employment levels as compared to the substantial improvement in Suffolk County. The North Amityville unemployment rates were higher, and labor participation rates were lower, than surrounding Suffolk County, with the North Amityville workforce more widely employed in jobs requiring less skill than the greater Suffolk County. Moreover, fewer North Amityville residents owned their own homes, while more were living in rental apartments paying higher rents. The following comparison of a broad range of social indicators and economic data shows how North Amityville, a depressed economic community, did not fare as well as Suffolk County.

POPULATION:
Table 1: Racial Composition

		1970		1990		Increase (Decrease)	
Suffolk County:	Total	1,124,950	100%	1,321,864	100%	196,914	18%
	White	1,066,429	95%	1,190,315	90%	123,886	12%
	Black	53,340	5%	82,910	6%	29,570	55%
	Other(a)	5,181	-	48,639	4%	43,458	838%
North Amityville:	Total	11,936	100%	13,849	100%	1,913	16%
	White	4,072	34%	2,403	17%	(1,669)	(41%)
	Black	7,768	66%	10,797	78%	3,029	39%
	Other	96	-	649	5%	553	576%

Source: 1970 U.S. Census, table P-1., 1990 U. S. Census, table 57.
Note (a): Other includes Natural Americans and Asians.

The total Suffolk County population grew by 18 percent between 1970 and 1990, to a total of 1,321,864, whereas by 1990, the North Amityville community reported growth of 16 percent to 13,849. While the population growth percentages were similar, the changes in their racial composition were not. In 1970, whites and blacks respectively represented 95.3 and 4.7 percent of Suffolk County's population. By 1990 the black component of Suffolk County's population had increased to 6 percent, while whites decreased to 90 percent; the non-white non-black population (termed other) rose from less than 1 percent to 4

13

percent. Blacks grew at a faster pace, increasing by 55 percent or 29,570, to 82,910. Whites, while increasing by 123,886 people, grew at a slower rate of 12 percent.

Between 1970 and 1990, as the total population of North Amityville increased, so did the concentration of blacks residents. In 1970, the North Amityville population was 34 percent white and 66 percent black. By 1990, the North Amityville population of 13,849 represented growth of 16 percent, with blacks accounting for all the growth. The white population had decreased by 41 percent, with those remaining representing only 17 percent of the North Amityville population. Blacks, however, increasing by 39 percent to 10,797 persons, now represented 78 percent of the population, making the concentrated black community of North Amityville more segregated from the rest of Suffolk County. In contrast, while Suffolk County as a whole appeared slightly more integrated, North Amityville and other Long Island communities where black majorities existed, such as Roosevelt, Hempstead Village, and Bellport, actually became more segregated.

FAMILY STRUCTURE:
Table 2: Family Composition (with children under 18 years of age)

		1970		1990		Increase (Decrease)	
Suffolk	Total Families	264,800	100%	340,593	100%	75,793	29%
County:	Husband/Wife	240,446	91%	282,081	83%	41,635	17%
	Male head	5,131	2%	14,399	4%	9,268	181%
	Female head	19,223	7%	44,113	13%	24,890	129%
	Persons per family	3.67		3.40		(.27)	(7%)
North	Total Families	2,679	100%	2,699	100%	20	1%
Amityville:	Husband/Wife	2,094	78%	1,662	62%	(432)	(21%)
	Male head	84	3%	189	7%	105	125%
	Female head	501	19%	848	31%	347	69%
	Persons per family	3.70		3.82		.12	3%

Source: 1970 U.S. Census Table P-1, 1990 Census Table 57 and Table 1.

Changes in family composition between 1970 and 1990 reflected greater structural weakening of the two-parent household in both North Amityville, and the surrounding Suffolk County. As shown in Table 2, single parent families rose 77 percent in North Amityville and 140 percent in Suffolk County as a whole. However, an example of two communities heading in opposite directions is that, between 1970 and 1990 two parent families decreased by 21 percent in North Amityville while growing by 17 percent for Suffolk County as a whole. By 1990, 17 percent of families with children in the greater Suffolk County had single parent households, compared to 9 percent two decades earlier. In North Amityville 1970 single-family households, were already at a high level of 22 percent of all households, growing to 38 percent by 1990.

In contrast to the 1990 family structure in Suffolk County where 87 percent of families with children under 18 years of age had a male present, a male presence was reported in only 69 percent of North Amityville families. Both represented a decrease from 1970, where 93 percent of Suffolk County families had a male present as compared to 81 percent of North Amityville families. The average 1970 North Amityville family size of 3.7 persons was comparable to Suffolk County, however, by 1990 family demographics had changed. Families with a husband and wife had decreased by 21 percent, male headed families increased by 125 percent, and families headed by females increased by 69 percent. While families with children under 18 in Suffolk County experienced 29 percent growth between 1970 and 1990, families in North Amityville increased by only 1 percent to 2,699. While there was little growth in total North Amityville families, the average 1990 family became larger, increasing by 3 percent from 1970 to 3.82 persons per family.

Table 3: Marital Status (those 14 years of age and older)

		1970		1990		Increase (Decrease)	
Suffolk	Total Males	369,092	100%	508,381	100%	139,289	38%
County:	Single Males	113,288	31%	205,480	40%	92,192	81%
	Married Males	255,804	69%	302,901	60%	47,097	18%
	Total Females	398,498	100%	544,293	100%	145,795	37%
	Single Females	136,612	34%	242,571	45%	105,959	78%
	Married Females	261,886	66%	301,722	55%	39,836	15%
North	Total Males	3,724	100%	4,258	100%	534	14%
Amityville:	Single Males	1,275	34%	2,298	54%	1,023	80%
	Married Males	2,449	66%	1,960	46%	(489)	(20%)
	Total Females	4,561	100%	5,303	100%	742	16%
	Single Females	1,899	42%	3,353	63%	1,454	77%
	Married Females	2,662	58%	1,950	37%	(712)	(27%)

Source: 1970 U.S.Census Table P-1, 1990 U.S. Census Table 57 and Table 1.

Integral to family structure stability is the marital status of men and women. In 1970, 69 percent of the males living in Suffolk County older than 14 years of age were married while 31 percent were single. Similarly, 34 percent of women were single with 66 percent married. By 1990, males had increased by 38 percent, with single males growing by 81 percent and married males, growing at a slower rate, increased by 18 percent. Single males over 14 now represented 40 percent of males, with married males falling to 60 percent. In similar fashion, by 1990 single females over 14 living in Suffolk County had grown by 78 percent, and now represented 45 percent of females. Married females growing at a slower 15 percent, decreased to 55 percent of Suffolk County females.

Between 1970 and 1990, single and married males and females over 14 years of age living in North Amityville followed a pattern similar to Suffolk County. The movement, however, was more dramatic. While Suffolk County males and females grew by 38 and 37 percent respectively, North Amityville males and females grew at a respectively slower 14 and 16 percent. However, the composition of that growth was very different from that of Suffolk County. Whereas Suffolk County experienced growth, albeit slower growth, in married males and females over 14, married males and females in North Amityville experienced significant declines between 1970 and 1990. While single males increased by 80

CHAPTER III

percent, married males decreased by 20 percent. Likewise, single North Amityville females increased by 77 percent, with married females decreasing by 27 percent. In 1970, 34 percent of males were single, with 66 percent married, while 42 percent of females were single and 58 percent married. By 1990, reflecting the decline in North Amityville married males and females, of the males, 54 percent were single and 46 percent were married, while 63 percent females were single and 37 percent were married. In twenty years, the structure of Suffolk County and North Amityville families had become very different. While married males and females in Suffolk County had decreased, 60 percent of males and 55 percent of females were still married. In contrast, only 46 percent of males and 37 percent of females living in North Amityville were married.

ACADEMIC ACHIEVEMENT:

If a correlation exists between academic achievement and higher family income, it may therefore be reasoned that those advancing to higher education have an opportunity to work in higher paying jobs. Such a correlation developed between 1970 and 1990, where differences in the pattern of school enrollment and in educational achievement between Suffolk County and the North Amityville community emerged.

Table 4: School Enrollment (3 years of age and older)

		1970		1990		Increase (Decrease)	
Suffolk	Preliminary	33,561	9%	28,516	8%	(5,045)	(15%)
County:	Elementary-H.S.	302,318	83%	218,985	63%	(83,333)	(28%)
	College	30,440	8%	100,187	29%	69,747	229%
	Total	366,319	100%	347,688	100%	18,631	5%
North	Preliminary	320	9%	182	5%	(138)	(43%)
Amityville:	Elementary-H.S.	3,201	86%	2,883	78%	(318)	(10%)
	College	195	5%	618	17%	423	217%
	Total	3,716	100%	3,683	100%	(33)	(1%)

Source: 1970 U.S. Census Table P-2, 1990 U.S. Census Table 3.

In 1970, Suffolk County and North Amityville exhibited similar patterns of school enrollment. Of the 366,319 persons over 3 years of age enrolled in Suffolk County schools, 9 percent were enrolled in preliminary schools, 83 percent were in elementary through high school, and 8 percent were attending college. By comparison, of the 3,716 North Amityville school enrollees, 9 percent attended preliminary schools, 86 percent were enrolled in elementary through high school, and 5 percent were attending college. By 1990, differing patterns appeared in those enrolled in elementary through high school and those attending college. In Suffolk County, of the 347,688 persons attending school, 8 percent were in preliminary schools, 63 percent were in elementary through high school, and 29 percent were attending college. Of the 3,683 students in North Amityville, 5 percent were in preliminary schools, 78 percent were enrolled in elementary or high school, and 17 percent were attending college. The enrollment distribution disparity became clearer by 1990, where 71 percent of Suffolk County school attendees were in high school or less, as compared to 83 percent in North Amityville. This resulted in a higher education enrollment gap, where 29 percent of those in Suffolk County attending college exceeded the 17 percent in North Amityville. An educational enrollment gap had developed despite the fact that those in North Amityville attending college grew by 217 percent between 1970 and 1990, keeping pace with the 229 percent growth in Suffolk County. The importance of the growth of college enrollment for both Suffolk County and North Amityville residents is that a correlation exists between higher levels of education and greater household income. That North Amityville growth in college enrollment kept pace with Suffolk County would indicate that increased future household incomes could be anticipated in North Amityville, providing that students remain attached to their community.

Table 5: Educational Attainment - over 25 years of age

		1970		1990		Increase (Decrease)	
Suffolk	8th Grade or less	123,459	21%	47,922	6%	(75,537)	(61%)
County:	9-12 gr. no diploma	115,312	20%	99,245	12%	(16,067)	(14%)
	High School Grad	212,082	36%	278,407	33%	66,325	31%
	College 1-3 yrs.	61,603	11%	222,606	26%	161,003	261%
	College Grad +	69,959	12%	195,333	23%	125,374	179%
	Total	582,415	100%	843,513	100%	261,098	45%
North	8th Grade or less	2,067	34%	839	10%	(1,228)	(59%)
Amityville:	9-12 gr. no diploma	1,591	26%	1,702	20%	111	7%
	High School Grad.	1,650	27%	2,912	34%	1,262	76%
	College 1-3 yrs.	493	8%	2,182	26%	1,689	343%
	College Grad +	346	5%	826	10%	480	139%
	Total	6,147	100%	8,461	100%	2,314	38%

Source: 1970 U.S. Census Table P-2, 1990 U.S. Census Tables 152 and 17.

In 1970, an educational attainment gap was developing between Suffolk County and North Amityville. While 52 and 51 percent of the respective 1970 Suffolk County and North Amityville populations had completed some level of schooling, 59 percent of those over 25 years of age in Suffolk County had graduated high school or gone on to higher education as compared to 40 percent in North Amityville. By 1990, while North Amityville showed improvement, the education attainment gap continued to widen. Those over 25 years of age having attained some level of education had grown to 64 and 61 percent of the respective Suffolk County and North Amityville populations, with 82 percent of those in Suffolk County having graduated high school and gone on to higher education as compared to 70 percent in North Amityville. Furthermore, those in Suffolk County over 25 years of age attending school increased by 45 percent between 1970 and 1990, as compared to 38 percent in North Amityville.

The importance of this education attainment gap is that it occurred when changes in the global economy restructured the job market from jobs requiring a lesser degree of education and skills to jobs requiring a higher level. While there was comparable growth in college and post college education attainment, the 36 percent of North Amityville residents attaining higher education levels still lagged behind the 49 percent in greater Suffolk County, drawing the correlation that a greater proportion of the North Amityville population was employed in lower paying jobs, resulting in lower family income.

CHAPTER III
WORKFORCE EMPLOYMENT:
A correlation was found to exist between the higher levels of educational enrollment and attainment levels achieved by Suffolk County residents and their higher workforce employment rates and greater representation in higher paying jobs. Similarly, North Amityville's lower level of educational enrollment and achievement levels resulted in lower employment rates and higher representation in lower paying jobs. In 1970, the 388,978 Suffolk County persons over 16 years of age in the workforce represented 35 percent of the population, as compared to 38 percent of North Amityville's population, or 4,515 persons. The composition of the respective workforce was also similar. Of note is the growing reliance on government employment in North Amityville, due to the relative stability of employment as well as a job that provides pension and health benefit.

Table 6: Workforce Employment - over 16 years of age

		1970		1990		Increase (Decrease)	
Suffolk	Private wage & salary	282,664	73%	497,060	76%	214,396	76%
County:	Government	81,801	21%	121,969	19%	40,168	49%
	Self-employed	24,513	6%	35,382	5%	10,869	44%
	Total	388,978	100%	654,411	100%	265,433	68%
North	Private wage & salary	3,336	74%	3,430	70%	94	3%
Amityville:	Government	1,021	23%	1,374	28%	353	35%
	Self-employed	158	3%	76	2%	(82)	(52%)
	Total	4,515	100%	4,880	100%	365	8%

Source: 1970 U.S Census Table P-3, 1990 U.S. Census Table 18, 1990 Census of Population-NYS Data Center

JOB SKILLS:
Employment of Suffolk County and North Amityville workers were comparable in most industry sectors, excepting for jobs in the professional, managerial and administrative categories. These jobs tend to require a higher degree of education, something achieved in greater percentages by the Suffolk County workforce. Conversely, service and machine operator jobs, often requiring a lower degree of education, were the two largest categories employing North Amityville residents.

Table 7: Employment by Industry Sector

	1970			
Industry Sector	Suffolk County		North Amityville	
Professional	71,418	18%	494	11%
Manager/Administrator	37,478	10%	176	4%
Sales	32,252	8%	123	3%
Clerical	67,721	17%	819	18%
Crafts/Construct/Mechanic	60,744	15%	551	12%
Machine Operators	34,573	9%	800	18%
Transportation Operators	15,156	4%	187	4%
Laborers	15,513	4%	275	6%
Farm	2,432	1%	44	1%
Service	49,160	13%	921	20%
Private Household	2,531	1%	125	3%
Total	388,978	100%	4,515	100%

Source: 1970 Census, table P-3, Labor Force Characteristics of the Population

By 1990, the differing levels of educational attainment between Suffolk County and North Amityville residents had resulted in recognizable differences in work force employment (Table 6). The 1990 Suffolk County labor force employment for those over 16 years old increased by 68 percent to 654,411, and now represented 50 percent of the Suffolk County population. North Amityville's labor force was not so fortunate. The 4,880 persons in 1990 working represented 35 percent of North Amityville's population, reflecting a dismal 8 percent employment growth from 1970. Additionally, those employed in private wage and salary jobs increased by only three percent, as compared to Suffolk County's 76 percent growth. Government employment increased by 35 percent; again lower than the 49 percent growth in Suffolk County. Entrepreneurs, the backbone of small business and critical to economic growth of any community was significantly different between Suffolk County and North Amityville. In Suffolk County, those self-employed increased by 44 percent between 1970 and 1990, while in North Amityville, self-employed individuals, already in short supply, decreased by 52 percent. Furthermore, the composition of the respective workforce also changed during the 20 years ending with 1990, and appears in the following analysis.

Table 7 (cont): Employment by Industry Sector

Industry Sector	1990 Suffolk County		North Amityville	
Professional	102,542	16%	453	9%
Manager/Administrator	88,832	13%	204	4%
Sales	108,303	16%	459	9%
Clerical	117,399	18%	1,049	22%
Crafts/Construct/Mechanics	77,943	12%	51	10%
Machine Operators	24,830	4%	302	6%
Transportation Operators	25,528	4%	370	8%
Laborers	20,125	3%	204	4%
Farm	8,253	1%	12	.5%
Service	78,804	12%	1,295	27%
Private Household	1,852	1%	20	.5%
Total	654,411	100%	4,880	100%

Source: 1990 U.S. Census, table 156 and table 23.

Not only did the growth between 1970 and 1990 of the North Amityville employment of over 16 year olds lag seriously behind Suffolk County, so did the distribution of jobs between the higher paying professional, managerial and administrative, crafts and construction sectors. These jobs tend to require a higher degree of education and skills, areas in which North Amityville failed to keep pace with Suffolk County. Suffolk County increased professional jobs by 44 percent, managerial and administrative by 137 percent and crafts and construction jobs by 28 percent. By comparison, North Amityville lost 8 percent of its professional jobs, increased managerial and administrative employment by only 16 percent and lost 7 percent of its crafts and construction employment. Even in occupations where a lower level of education would be acceptable, such as clerical and service, Suffolk County grew at 73 and 60 percent respectively, while North Amityville reported growth of 28 percent for clerical and 41 percent for service.

Not only did the North Amityville labor force lag behind Suffolk County in growth of higher paying jobs, but North Amityville also reported a higher degree of unemployment, when comparing those employed to those who are not.

Table 8: Employment Status - Male and Female - 16 years of age and older

		1970		1990		Increase (Decrease)	
Suffolk	Males employed	259,862	67%	368,144	56%	108,282	42%
County:	Females employed	129,116	33%	286,267	44%	157,151	122%
	Total	388,978	100%	654,411	100%	265,433	68%
North	Males employed	2,432	54%	2,648	54%	216	9%
Amityville:	Females employed	2,083	46%	2,232	46%	149	7%
	Total	4,515	100%	4,880	100%	365	8%

Source: 1970 U.S. Census Table P-3, 1990 U.S. Census Tables 22 and 156.

In 1970, of the 388,978 persons over 16 years of age employed in Suffolk County, 67 percent were male and 33 percent females, a 2-to-1 ratio. For the 4,515 persons over 16 employed in North Amityville, 54 percent were male and 46 percent female, a 1.17 to 1 ratio. By 1990, males in the Suffolk County workforce had increased by 42 percent, yet fell to 56 percent of the employment base. Females, however, increased by 122 percent, while improving their labor force participation to 44 percent. The male to female ratio in the workforce had narrowed to 1.27 to 1. By contrast, North Amityville lagged seriously behind Suffolk County with a meager 9 percent growth in employed males and a 7 percent growth in employed females. The result was that males and females employed in North Amityville respectively remained at 54 and 46 percent of the labor force. As female headed families increased regionally, more females participated in the labor force change in Suffolk County, as did in North Amityville. An important distinction is that while females represented a major share of the increase in the Suffolk County workforce, North Amityville females did not. The ratios remained the same; in as the North Amityville employment base grew only slightly.

As would also be expected, the relationship existing between the employment and unemployment status of males and females over 16 years of age was disproportionately favorable to Suffolk County over North Amityville.

Table 9: Unemployed Compared to Workforce (a)

		1970		1990		Increase (Decrease)	
Suffolk	Total Workforce	403,170	- - -	687,030	- - -	283,860	- - -
County:	Male unemployed	7,863	2.0%	18,006	2.6%	10,143	129%
	Female unemployed	6,329	1.5%	14,613	2.1%	8,284	131%
	Total	14,192	3.5%	32,619	4.7%	18,427	130%
North	Total Workforce	4,705	- - -	5,711	- - -	1,006	- - -
Amityville:	Male unemployed	113	2.4%	595	10.4%	482	427%
	Female unemployed	77	1.6%	236	4.1%	159	206%
	Total	190	4.0%	831	14.5%	641	337%

Source: 1970 U.S. Census Table P-3, 1990 U.S. Census Tables18 and 154.
Note (a): Workforce defined as employed plus unemployed.

The 1970 Suffolk County unemployed represented 3.5 percent of the workforce, with males approximately 3 percent of their workforce and females 5 percent. Similarly, the North Amityville unemployed were 4 percent of the employment base, with males 5 percent of the male workforce and females 4 percent. By 1990, the Suffolk County unemployed modestly increased to 4.7 percent of the workforce, while North Amityville's unemployment rate more than tripled. The unemployment status of Suffolk County males and females in 1990 each increased to 5 percent of their respective employment bases, with unemployed males and females increasing respectively by 129 and 131 percent from 1970. In stark contrast, North Amityville's male unemployed increased by 427 percent, and females by 206 percent. Significant is that between 1970 and 1990 the North Amityville unemployment rate grew approximately ten times faster than Suffolk County's rate. Also important was the fact that the North Amityville male unemployment rate by 1990 was 4 times greater than the Suffolk County male unemployment rate.

A comparison between employed and unemployed reveals how poorly North Amityville had fared as compared to Suffolk County. Between 1970 and 1990, the ratio of the 265,433 new jobs created by the Suffolk County economy to the increase of 18,427 unemployed was 14.4 to 1. The reverse was true for North Amityville, where the net job loss of 276 resulted in a workforce where 1.76 persons were unemployed for every one working. As a result, the ratio of employed to unemployed in North Amityville, as compared to Suffolk County, got progressively worse between 1970 and 1990. In 1970, the Suffolk County ratio was 27.4 persons employed to every person unemployed, with a 23.8 to 1 ratio in North Amityville. By 1990, the Suffolk County ratio narrowed to 20 to 1, while North Amityville plummeted to 5.9 to 1. North Amityville had become a pocket of lower economic activity surrounded by an economically vibrant Suffolk County.

FAMILY INCOME:

The socioeconomic infrastructure of North Amityville has weakened. Residents lagged behind Suffolk County in academic attainment and job skills, resulting in a workforce that was forced to accept lower paying jobs. Furthermore, North Amityville had far more single parent households headed by females, and fewer families headed by both husbands and wives. With workers lacking the required skills for higher paying jobs, and having fewer wage earners in their families, a drawn conclusion is that North Amityville family income would be less than that of Suffolk County families. The following tables reflect how family income in North Amityville, while improving between 1970 and 1990, still fell further behind family income growth for Suffolk County.

Table 10: Nominal Family Income

Nominal Family Income	1970			
	Suffolk County Families		North Amityville Families	
$0 - $5,000	26,387	10%	510	19%
$5,000-$10,000	63,832	24%	894	33%
$10,000-$15,000	90,894	34%	759	27%
$15,000-$25,000	67,562	25%	484	18%
$25,000-$50,000	15,396	6%	77	3%
$50,000 and over	2,101	1%	0	0%
Total	266,172	100%	2,724	100%

Table 10 (cont): Nominal Family Income

1990

Nominal Family Income	Suffolk County Families		North Amityville Families	
$0-$5,000	4,730	1%	70	2%
$5,000-$10,000	6,407	2%	119	4%
$10,000-$15,000	10,536	3%	173	6%
$15,000-$25,000	27,903	8%	512	17%
$25,000-$50,000	105,383	31%	1,201	38%
$50,000 and over	188,652	55%	1,005	33%
Total	343,611	100%	3,080	100%

Source: 1970 U.S. Census table P-4, Income characteristics of the population; 1990 U.S. Census table 148, Income of Households, Families and Persons; New York State Data Center, Department of Economic Development Summary Tape.

In 1970, the 52 percent of North Amityville families represented at the lower income categories exceeded the 34 percent of Suffolk County families earning $10,000 or less. Few families earned over $25,000, with 7 percent of Suffolk County families earning in excess of $25,000, as compared to 3 percent for North Amityville families. Furthermore, no North Amityville families earned over $50,000, while 1 percent of Suffolk County families did. By 1990, correlating with improving educational attainment, economic conditions improved to where only 3 percent of Suffolk County families and 6 percent of North Amityville families were earning less than $10,000. Conditions also improved to where 86 percent of Suffolk County families earned in excess of $25,000, followed by 71 percent of North Amityville families. In part because more residents attended or graduated college, Suffolk County families earning over $50,000 improved from 1 percent in 1970 to 55 percent in 1990. Reflecting a lower percent of college attendees and graduates, North Amityville families earning over $50,000 per year, while improving from 0 percent in 1970 to 33 percent by 1990, still lagged behind Suffolk County.

Family mean and median income distribution variances also existed between Suffolk County and North Amityville, and are presented in the following table.

Table 11: Mean and Median Family (Nominal and Real) Income

	1970		1990	
	Mean	Median	Mean	Median
Suffolk County:				
Nominal $	$13,382	$12,084	$61,789	$53,247
Real $ (1)	$34,490	$31,144	$47,530	$40,959
North Amityville:				
Nominal $	$10,240	$9,446	$42,764	$37,544
Real $ (1)	$26,391	$24,345	$32,895	$28,880

Source:1970 U.S.Census table P-4, 1990 U.S.Census table 148, NYS Data Center, File 3.
Note (1): Based on 1984 CPI as the base year.

The 1970 North Amityville mean and median family incomes, expressed in both nominal and real dollars, were respectively 77 and 78 percent of their Suffolk County equivalent. This gap became progressively worse by 1990. The Suffolk County nominal mean and median family incomes experienced a respective 362 and 341 percent growth between 1970 and 1990, while mean and median incomes expressed in real dollars grew by 38 and 32 percent respectively. The growth of North Amityville's mean and median family incomes, expressed in nominal dollars lagged behind at 318 and 297 percent, with mean and median income expressed in real dollars also lagging behind with growth rates of 25 and 19 percent respectively. The North Amityville mean and median family incomes expressed in both nominal and real dollars had now having fallen to 69 and 71 percent of their Suffolk County equivalents.

HOUSING:

As would be expected, with the additional costs of home ownership, including down-payment requirements, the lower mean and median family incomes in North Amityville impacted the incidence of home ownership.

Table 12: Occupied Housing Units

		1970		1990		Increase (Decrease)	
Suffolk	Total occupied units	312,050	100%	424,719	100%	112,669	36%
County:	Owner occupied	245,818	79%	340,347	80%	94,529	38%
	Renter occupied	66,232	21%	84,372	20%	18,140	27%
North	Total occupied units	3,185	100%	3,991	100%	806	25%
Amityville:	Owner occupied	2,320	73%	2,815	71%	495	21%
	Renter occupied	865	27%	1,176	29%	311	36%

Source: 1970 U.S. Census Table H-1, 1990 U.S. Census Tables 15 and 152.

In 1970, of the total occupied housing units in Suffolk County, 79 percent were owner occupied and 21 percent renter occupied. Of North Amityville's total occupied housing units, 73 percent were owner occupied with 27 percent renter occupied. By 1990, total Suffolk County housing units had increased by 36 percent, with 84 percent of the increase owner occupied units, and 16 percent renter occupied. In North Amityville, the total occupied housing units increased by 25 percent, with 61 percent of the increase owner occupied units, and 39 percent renter occupied. While Suffolk County experienced a respective 38 and 27 percent increase in owner and renter occupied housing units, the reverse was happening in North Amityville where owner and renter occupied housing units increased by 21 and 36 percent respectively. Suffolk County's growth in owner occupied housing units had exceeded that of renter occupied units, while the opposite was occurring in North Amityville where renter occupied housing units grew at a faster rate than owner occupied units.

In a trend that continued between 1970 and 1990, the 1970 median gross rent in North Amityville of $188, was higher than the Suffolk County median gross rent of $147. By 1990, the median gross rent of North Amityville had increased to $879, as compared to Suffolk County's $802 (1970 U.S. Census, table H-1, 1990 U.S. Census table 15).

CHAPTER III

Interestingly, despite significantly lower incomes, renters in North Amityville continued to pay a higher rent than Suffolk County as a whole.

SUMMARY:

Of all the socioeconomic indicators discussed above, family structure and academic attainment, workforce participation, jobs skills, household income, and home ownership, North Amityville started from a less favorable position compared to Suffolk County as a whole. The 20-year period covered by this analysis is especially interesting since it coincides with the emergence and maturity of the global economy. As compared to Suffolk County the global economy impact on North Amityville was that North Amityville:

(1)   become a more concentrated and racially segregated black community, despite experiencing population growth at approximately the same rate as Suffolk County;

(2)   experienced a steep decrease in families with a male and female present, and had more families headed by women than men;

(3)   had a breakdown of traditional family structure, where there are now more single males and females than married males and females;

(4)   had slower growth in college enrollments, with greater student enrollment in elementary and high school;

(5)   slower growth in post-secondary education attainment;

(6)   had a decrease in self-employed entrepreneurs, a decrease in private sector employment, and an increase in government employment;

(7)   had a decrease in higher paying professional, craft, construction, and machine operator jobs, and an increase in lower paying service and sales jobs;

(8)   experienced a much sharper growth in both male and female unemployment;

(9)   had a growth in nominal family income, yet a majority of families were still earning nominal income below $38,000 as compared to approximately $53,000 for Suffolk County;

(10)   had mean and median real family income grow at a slower rate than Suffolk County's;

(11)   had a proportionate decrease in owner occupied housing units and an increase in renter occupied units; the opposite being true for Suffolk County.

Overall, despite experiencing some growth between 1970 and 1990, the skills required by the global economy, combined with the deindustrialization of Long Island economy impacted North Amityville, resulting in the community economically falling further behind Suffolk County.

The impact of the global economy did not stop with 1990, but continues to impact the current Long Island economy. How that impact was felt will be illustrated by the following analysis of three Long Island communities. The first of these is Huntington Station, a multi-cultural community of color.

CHAPTER III

Chapter IV

HUNTINGTON STATION:
RISE AND FALL OF A COMMERCIAL CENTER

Huntington Station, located in the Town of Huntington and the County of Suffolk, is similar to most downtown areas struggling to revitalize themselves. The current economic base has evolved over the past forty-five years, first impacted by the unfulfilled promises of the enacted Urban Renewal Programs of the 1960's, then by economic development decisions, demographic changes and a shifting regional economic base. What happened during this period is seen through the recollections of Dolores Thompson (Dee to most) who has been living in, and working to make Huntington Station better since she moved there some 55 years ago.

I first met Dee Thompson during my tenure as project director for the Long Island Neighborhood Development Initiative (LINDI), a collaboration funded by Horace and Amy Hagedorn, Citibank, The Long Island Community Foundation, The Rauch Foundation, and the Long Island Development Corp. The LINDI collaboration members believed that a lack of information and access to resources outside their community limited community based organizations from turning their development goals into viable projects. LINDI committed funds to hire a project director with strong experience in community and economic development to assist local groups in strengthening their capacity to succeed with short and long-term projects.

Dee Thompson had sought technical and financial assistance from LINDI to help her find a permanent home for her organization, the Huntington Station Enrichment Center (HSEC). Dee was, and still is, the executive director of the HSEC. She brought vision with her plans; strong management experience, has shown that she has perseverance, seldom fails, has community support, with most people thinking highly of her. She has been a permanent fixture in the social fabric of Huntington Station, and what follows is a glimpse into her life and her community.

As have many Long Islanders before her, Huntington Station resident Dee Thompson was originally a New York City resident. She was born in Brooklyn's Cumberland Hospital over 70 years ago, living on Pacific Street during her early years with her mother and father. Her father worked for Gillette Camera (Kodak) and her mother was a homemaker, a seamstress, and played piano for her church. When Dee was ready for school, her family moved to Jamaica Queens to attend Public School 116.[30]

As many Long Islanders of the post World War II era, what prompted Dee's family's move to Long Island was to find a better quality of life, a goal made very clear when Dee's mother was robbed near their Jamaica home. In 1946, shortly after the robbery, and while Dee was in junior high school, the family decided to move to Long Island and purchased a home in Woodbury to be near other family members. Quality of Life was so important that Dee's family left a neighborhood with local schools to Woodbury that had no schools. To attend school, Dee was bussed daily to junior and senior high school in Huntington Station.

---

[30] Dee Thompson, Personal Interview, 23 May 2006.

CHAPTER IV

At the time that Dee Thompson's family moved to Long Island, Woodbury was developing as a housing resource for the workforce needed by Huntington Station, which was a regional population center and an important generator of Long Island economic activity. Dee recalls that during her time in school she experienced little racism.

It was in high school that Dee met her husband, whom she married when she turned 18 years of age. They purchased a home in Huntington Station, at that time a shell home that they built out and completed. While land was affordable in both Huntington Station and Lloyd Harbor, an upscale community, Dee believed that she and her husband were shown only Huntington Station, but believes that the reasons had more to do with economics rather than race, but can't be sure. While land was less expensive in Lloyd Harbor, Dee and her husband were only shown Huntington Station because land was less expensive there and at that time there was no affordable housing for people of color.

During her early marriage, Dee recalls that race was not a hindering factor for two reasons. The first was that the Huntington Town police force needed black officers and hired her husband, who later became a Suffolk County police officer after the Huntington Town police force was absorbed by Suffolk County. The second was that her husband was a member of the then dominant Republican Party, allowing Dee to move around a natural network of Long Islanders that was built around politics.

During her 24 years of marriage, which ended in divorce, Dee raised a family of two children, a son and a daughter. The son died in an accident in the mountains of Tennessee when the truck he was driving crashed. Dee still doesn't know the cause of death or full details of the incident, and since the accident occurred in the south Dee concluded that getting good answers would be difficult. Her younger child was a daughter Tracy, who is now vice-president of human resources for Verizon Telephone. Tracy was also chair of the Town of Huntington Planning Board, served ten years on the local Elwood School Board, and was a candidate for the Huntington Town Board. Tracy clearly benefited from Dee's experiences.

After graduating Huntington High School Dee went to work for a local answering service for doctors, followed by employment at the Long Island offices of New York Telephone, eventually rising to supervisor. She held that position for 30 years, including the tumultuous period during the dismantling of AT&T and realignment of New York Telephone.

While Dee's career at New York Telephone appeared to be without obstacles, it was not always without challenges. Dee began her career as an assistant manager working her way up to manager. It wasn't until she wanted to move up to group manager that she recalled experiencing racism and sexism. This impacted her ability to grow professionally and get promoted to group manager, which was the quickest way to get to the job she really wanted which was the New York City-based chief of operator services. However, that position was not open at the time, so to get a promotion and pay increase, Dee had to take a non-traditional job career path to foreman, which required her to climb telephone polls. Fortunately, before she was promoted to foreman, the chief of operator services became available, and Dee being promoted to that position.

In recalling her past New York Telephone work experience, Dee remembered a question from the New York City District Manager, a white male, about the most challenging aspect of the chief of operator services job. Dee said it was her being black and being in charge of mostly black workers. Since she developed professionally in the white world of the New York Telephone Long Island workplaces of Huntington, Smithtown and Wantagh, when she began at the New York City offices Dee found that the black employees distrusted her because they thought of her as a token black manager. Dee overcame those workplace obstacles and remained in New York City until her retirement in 1986.

After retirement, Dee looked around her Huntington Station neighborhood and determined that there were unmet community needs. She was concerned about how the urban renewal programs had decimated downtown Huntington Station, especially during her early years as a resident, mother, and taxpayer. She developed a community based needs assessment of Huntington Station, including the welfare to work program, and found that without training few doors opened for people of color. She researched the quality of training for people of color as compared to the white population, wondering why people of color were not getting academic scholarships to attend college, as compared to those people of color who received sports scholarships. She was concerned that most black children were put in special education programs, not because they needed it but because that is where they were placed. Dee believed that these children were not getting the education they needed to succeed. She also found that schools were not encouraging black children to go to college unless it was for sports, while in terms of academics, black children were encouraged to go to trade schools. With a blue-color pre-global based economy, this made absolute sense. But as with so many communities nationally, including Long Island, the global economy quickly altered workplace needs. Intuitively it became obvious changes were occurring in the economic foundation of Long Island, but identifying the root causes was elusive.

Dee, like many Long Islanders didn't know why these imbalances existed, but would not ignore the fact that they did. She concluded that additional voices were needed, and in 1986 became involved in the Town of Huntington Branch of the NAACP, becoming its president in 1994, a position she holds today.

Dee also turned her attention to educational resources for the children of Huntington Station and called for a meeting of the Huntington Library Board of Directors. She observed that Huntington Station was not only without a library, but that there was no access to computers and educational supportive resources for people of color. The result was Dee's founding of the Huntington Station Enrichment Center, a community based organization with the mission of job and computer training, job placement services for the community, resume building, dress for success, and employment training. The first location was at the library. Today, the organization remains as an important part of Huntington Station.

Dee devotes time to black males, and those who were recently incarcerated, because she believed then, and still does, that this is where there is a great-unmet need. She still gets letters from those in prison asking for help and stability after they are released, and continues to meet with prisoners concerned about what they will do after prison, especially about getting jobs. Dee also bridges the gap between black parents and white school officials by advocating for parents concerned about inequitable punishments for their children, bringing reason to often-misunderstood impressions. What matters most to Dee is fairness.

The history of Dee Thompson's Huntington Station, how it began, what significant events framed its future, what it looked like before she moved in, and why it looks as it does today follows.

CHAPTER IV

Huntington Station's emergence as a population and commercial center began 138 years ago and can be directly attributed to the expansion of the Long Island Rail Road (LIRR), which established a depot in 1867 on the site of the present station. As is often the case, the railroad brought commerce and people to the communities along its right-of-way. Thus, development came to eastern Long Island, and in particular to Huntington Station, where hotels, a bank, a post office, a racetrack, and two to three story buildings on both sides of New York Avenue were built to cater to both the needs of travelers, and to the eastern migrating population. These buildings provided space for offices, and convenience retail and service establishments. Goods and services offered included: coal, lumber and feed merchants, a bicycle shop, a barber, a shoe repair store, meat and poultry purveyors, a drug store, a general and sundry store, a bakery, a grocery store, an auto repair garage, and a ready to wear clothing store.[31] Huntington Station had become an important commercial center of western Suffolk County.

From its inception, Huntington Station became a transportation hub. Initially, stagecoaches linked up with scheduled arrivals of LIRR trains as they headed east, ultimately replaced by horse-drawn trolleys, and they in turn by electric trolleys and motorized buses. By 1910 a new LIRR station and underpass were built, with the station becoming the focal point of community and commercial activity. This encouraged the next generation of business activity to flourish. Over the next 50 years new merchants arrived providing goods and services to Huntington Station residents such as; department and sundry stores; a movie theater; more banks; several pharmacies; funeral homes; florists; jewelers; haberdashers; hardware and building supply stores; deli's, restaurants, bars and grills; fruit, vegetable and grocery stores; stationary and ice-cream stores; furniture stores; and other convenience stores and family-owned businesses.[32]

While merchants were meeting the demand for convenience shopping by the area's increasing population, Huntington Station was becoming an important manufacturing center for Suffolk County. A 1952 Huntington Town Chamber of Commerce listing of the 80 companies in the Town of Huntington was heavily weighted towards manufacturing. Employing 2,600 persons, these businesses produced station wagon bodies; lumber and building supplies; electronics; machine shops; sand and gravel; welding and iron works; ice and fuel; aerospace components; concrete; fishing; plastics and injection molding; tool and die; and pickle production. The workforce also included 339 persons employed by the electric, telephone and municipal water utilities.[33]

By the end of 1960, Huntington Station's economic growth had placed it at the top of the ten Suffolk County communities having the greatest number of manufacturers, wholesalers, and retailers. In 1961, Huntington Station, with over 6.6 percent of Suffolk County's 8,100 businesses, maintained that top ten ranking. According to a report compiling rankings by Dun and Bradstreet, the 532 Huntington Station businesses exceeded those in Babylon, Bay Shore, Lindenhurst, Huntington, Patchogue, Amityville, Riverhead, East Northport and Copiague.

All of that growth came to a halt during the 1960s. Under the rationalization of urban renewal, the 86 businesses surrounding the railroad station, and comprising the economic center and vital core of Huntington Station, were demolished. Conceptually, the displaced and relocated businesses were to be replaced by a modern shopping center with adequate

---

[31] Alfred Sforza, *Portrait of a Small Town* (New York: Maple Hill Press, 1996) p. 24-35.
[32] Ibid, p. 35-58.
[33] Huntington Township Chamber of Commerce. *Industries in Huntington Township.*
   (Huntington, New York 1952).

off-street parking. Additional office space was to be provided, while industrial uses eliminated. Housing was also impacted, with the urban renewal plan calling for the displacement of over 100 households, and the construction of new single-family housing and garden apartments capable of accommodating nearly 275 families.[34]

The urban renewal plan adopted by the Huntington Town Board was guided by several factors. These were, (a) that the projected LIRR rider-ship would double from 23,000 riders in 1963 to 46,000 by 1980; (b) that 10.27 acres would be required for commuter parking; (c) that relieving the congestion in the vicinity of the station was a pressing public need for the Town to act upon;[35] and (d) that the "land proposed for commercial use represented a reduction from existing allocation, in keeping with the transformation of the Huntington Station area from a regional shopping area to one predominantly servicing the local neighborhoods." It was believed that traffic congestion, lack of adequate and convenient parking spaces, and a lack of room for commercial expansion and modernization contributed to a decline of the commercial area. Ironically, despite Huntington Station's commercial district being anchored by a modern regional shopping center with ample off-street parking on New York Avenue, the prevailing planning policy as discussed in items (a)-(d) above, prevented Huntington Station from becoming a shopping destination of regional scale.[36]

Unfortunately the urban renewal plan failed to deliver on its vision. Rather than centralizing the commercial activity in a new neighborhood commercial district, the process of urban renewal eliminated the economic center of Huntington Station, replacing it with hundreds of commuter parking spaces, while decentralizing business activity elsewhere. The widening of New York Avenue, by the nearly 130 feet required for the four traffic lanes under the railroad overpass, separated the communities on the east and west side of New York Avenue. The failure to install the envisioned landscaped dividing mall on New York Avenue made crossing it unsafe and pedestrian unfriendly, and geographically divided the neighborhood and eroded Huntington Station's sense of community.

The Town of Huntington Planning Board, understanding the problems caused by Urban Renewal and the widening of New York Avenue, adopted a Comprehensive Plan Update in April 1993. The Planning Board recognized that the original 1965 Comprehensive Plan "classified Huntington Station as a Secondary Retail Center. Thus, the Update recognized that urban renewal efforts had altered the character of the area to the point where it no longer functioned, and was no longer perceived as a village center in the same vein as Greenlawn or East Northport."[37]

Compounding the economic impact of the failed urban renewal polices of the 1960's and 1970's on Huntington Station was the changing world economy. Subsequently, between 1980 and 2000, Long Island experienced the deindustrialization of its manufacturing base, caused in part by the contraction of the region's defense industry. Similar to the effects on North Amityville, this contraction, felt especially by Long Island's many machine shops, led to workforce reductions impacting much of the regions less skilled and less educated workers. At the same time, influenced largely by the globalization of economic activity between 1970 and 1990, in a trend that continued well beyond 1990's, the

[34] Office of Urban Renewal, Town of Huntington. *Facts About LIFT Project No. 1.* (Town of Huntington, 1966).
[35] Huntington Town Board. *General Neighborhood Renewal Plan, Huntington Station Area.* (Huntington, New York Nov. 1962), p. 15.
[36] Ibid, p. 10.
[37] The Town of Huntington. Report On The Huntington Station Moratorium Area.

demand for more skilled and more educated workers was growing in Long Island's high technology industries, and in the growing financial and banking sector. What remains to be determined is how Huntington Station, a culturally and ethnically diverse African-American, Hispanic and White community, fared between 1990 and 2000 as compared to the surrounding Suffolk County.

What would be the impact of this period of industrial and economic restructuring on the Huntington Station workforce and related economy? What would be the cost to the community of the loss of jobs that required a lower level of education, such as blue-collar manufacturing and clerical? Would Huntington Station's residents be able to achieve the education and skills necessary for employment in the emerging and higher paid technology jobs, such as specialized financial services, and computer and telecommunication technology and their related commercial applications? Would the global economy and changes in technology, now requiring more intellectual skills from the workforce, impact the correlation existing between education and family income as compared to past years? Would Huntington Station be similar to other primarily African-American and Hispanic communities, which tend to have inadequate support structures for families; often having families living in homes where lower property tax bases are inadequate to fund financially strapped educational systems; resulting in communities often lagging behind whites in educational attainment, employment, and income? The result for some contemporary American communities is that the income gap has widened between the haves and have-nots. Would Huntington Station have the same experience and lag behind Suffolk County?

The above questions will be explored by comparing Huntington Station, a multi-cultural African-American, Hispanic, and White community, with the surrounding primarily White, and economically more prosperous Suffolk County.

HUNTINGTON STATION: FORTY YEARS AFTER URBAN RENEWAL

The 10 years between 1990 and 2000 brought socioeconomic changes to the New York City metropolitan area, including the culturally and ethnically diverse African-American, Hispanic, and White community of Huntington Station. Huntington Station continues to have a large Black and Hispanic population, while experiencing growth in the Asian and Pacific Islander populations. Several indices point to Huntington Station's slower growth; as compared to the economic development that has characterized Suffolk County. Despite Huntington Station's single parent headed families growing at a pace 40 percent slower than Suffolk County, the concentration of single parent families in Huntington Station continued to outpace Suffolk County. In Huntington Station, single headed families increased to where they now represent 1 in 4 families, or 26.3 percent of all Huntington Station families. This is 36 percent greater than in Suffolk County, where 19.2 percent of families are headed by single persons and now represent 1 in 5 families. The educational enrollment in advanced grades is somewhat comparable to Suffolk County, with overall educational attainment levels in Huntington Station keeping pace. This, in part, explains Huntington Station's similar employment levels as compared to Suffolk County. The Huntington Station unemployment and labor participation rates were comparable to surrounding Suffolk County, with Huntington Station's workforce widely employed in jobs requiring skills similar to those in greater Suffolk County. However, fewer Huntington Station residents own their own homes, with more living in rental apartments and paying rents comparable to those charged in Suffolk County. The following comparison of a broad range of social indicators and economic data shows how Huntington Station, a community recovering from urban renewal, fared nearly as well as Suffolk County.

POPULATION
Table 1: Racial Composition

		1990		2000		Increase (Decrease)	
Suffolk	Total	1,321,864	100%	1,419,369	100%	97,505	7.4%
County:	White	1,190,315	90.0%	1,200,755	84.6%	10,440	.9%
	Black	82,910	6.3%	98,553	6.9%	15,643	18.9%
	Other (a)	48,639	3.7%	120,061	8.5%	71,422	146.8%
	Hispanic (of any race)	87,852	6.6%	149,411	10.5%	61,559	70.1%
Huntington	Total	28,247	100%	29,910	100%	1,663	5.9%
Station:	White	23,091	81.8%	21,401	71.5%	(1,690)	(7.3%)
	Black	3,596	12.7%	3,459	11.6%	(137)	(3.8%)
	Other	1,560	5.5%	5,050	16.9%	3,490	223.7%
	Hispanic (of any race)	3,377	12.0%	6,802	22.7%	3,425	101.4%

Source: 1990 U.S. Census, Table DP-1., 2000 U. S. Census, Table DP-1.
Note (a): Other includes Natural Americans, Asians and Pacific Islanders.

The total Suffolk County population grew by 7.4 percent between 1990 and 2000, to a total of 1,419,369, whereas by 2000, the Huntington Station community reported growth of 5.9 percent to 29,910. While the population growth percentages were similar, the changes in their racial composition were not. In 1990, whites and blacks respectively represented 90.0 and 6.3 percent of Suffolk County's population. By 2000, the black component of Suffolk County's population had increased slightly to 6.9 percent, while whites decreased to 84.6 percent. The non-white non-black population (termed other) rose exponentially by 146.8%, from 3.7 percent to 8.5 percent. Blacks grew at a faster pace, increasing by 18.9 percent or 15,643 persons to 98,553, while Whites, increasing by 10,440 people, grew marginally by .9 percent. The Hispanic population showed dramatic growth between 1990 and 2000. In 1990 Hispanics represented 6.6 percent of the Suffolk County population. This grew by 70.1 percent by 2000, with the 149,411 Hispanics representing 10.5 percent of the 2000 Suffolk County population.

Between 1990 and 2000, Huntington Station's population increased. Decreases were reported in both white and black residents, with other residents accounting for all the growth. In 1990, the Huntington Station population was 81.7 percent white and 12.7 percent black. By 2000, the Huntington Station population of 29,910 grew by 5.9 percent. The white population decreased by 7.3 percent, now representing 71.5 percent of the 2000 Huntington Station population. Others, including Asian and Pacific Islanders, increased by 223.7 percent to 5,050 persons, and now represented 16.9 percent of the population. Blacks, while decreasing 3.8 percent to 3,459, were now 11.6 percent of Huntington Station's population, making the black community of Huntington Station more concentrated than the rest of Suffolk County. The Hispanic community of Huntington Station exhibited significant growth between 1990 and 2000. In 1990, the 3,377 Hispanics represented 12.0 percent of the population, growing by 101.4 percent, or 3,425 persons, to where the 6,802 Hispanics now represented 22.7 percent of the 2000 Huntington Station community. Both in numbers and percentage of the community, Hispanics have become the largest minority population in both Huntington Station and Suffolk County.

FAMILY STRUCTURE
Table 2: Family Composition (with children under 18 years of age)

		1990		2000		Increase (Decrease)	
Suffolk	Total Families	340,593	100%	360,422	100%	19,829	5.8%
County:	Husband/Wife	282,081	82.8%	291,098	80.8%	9,017	3.2%
	Male head	14,399	4.2%	18,665	5.2%	4,266	29.6%
	Female head	44,113	13.0%	50,659	14.0%	6,546	14.8%
	Persons per Household	3.04		2.96		(.08)	(2.6)%
Huntington	Total Families	7,257	100%	7,190	100%	(67)	(.9%)
Station:	Husband/Wife	5,521	76.1%	5,296	73.7%	(225)	(4.1%)
	Male head	414	5.7%	502	6.9%	88	21.3%
	Female head	1,322	18.2%	1,392	19.4%	70	5.3%
	Persons per Household	2.93		3.06		.13	4.4%

Source: 1990 U.S. Census Table DP-1, 2000 Census Table DP-1.

Changes in family composition between 1990 and 2000 reflected similar structural weakening of the two-parent family in both Huntington Station and surrounding Suffolk County. As shown in Table 2, despite Huntington Station single parent families growing by 26.6 percent, that growth rate was nearly 40 percent less than Suffolk County's 44.4 percent. However, an example of two communities heading in somewhat different directions is that between 1990 and 2000 two parent families with children under 18 decreased by 4.1 percent in Huntington Station, while increasing by 3.2 percent in Suffolk County as a whole. By 2000, 19.2 percent of families with children in greater Suffolk County had single parent families, as compared to 17.2 percent one decade earlier, an 11.6 percent increase. This compares to the 23.9 percent of 1990 Huntington Station families that were headed by single persons. This group grew larger by 2000, growing by 10 percent to 26.3 percent of Huntington Station families.

In contrast to the 2000 family structure in Suffolk County, where 86.0 percent of families with children under 18 years of age had a male present, a male presence was reported in only 80.6 percent of Huntington Station families. Both represented a marginal decrease from 1990, where 87.0 percent of Suffolk County families had a male present as compared to 81.8 percent of Huntington Station families. Additionally, the average 1990 Huntington Station household size of 2.93 persons was 3.6 percent less crowded than the 3.04 persons in the average Suffolk County household. However by 2000, Huntington Station households became more crowded. Families in Huntington Station with both a husband and wife present had decreased by 4.1 percent, male headed families increased by 21.3 percent, and families headed by females increased by 5.3 percent. In Suffolk County, families with children under 18 experienced a 5.8 percent growth between 1990 and 2000, while families in Huntington Station decreased by .9 percent to 7,190. While there was growth in total Suffolk County families, the average 2000 household became smaller, decreasing by 2.6 percent from 3.04 persons in 1990 to 2.96 persons. Despite families in Huntington Station decreasing by .9 percent, they became more crowded, growing by 4.4 percent to 3.06 persons in 2000.

Table 3: Marital Status (those 14 years of age and older)

		1990		2000		Increase (Decrease)	
Suffolk	Total Males	508,381	100%	516,143	100%	7,762	1.5%
County:	Single Males	205,480	40.4%	193,684	37.5%	(11,796)	(5.7)%
	Married Males	302,901	59.6%	322,459	62.5%	19,558	6.5 %
	Total Females	544,293	100%	589,515	100%	45,222	8.3%
	Single Females	242,571	44.6%	267,056	45.3%	24,485	10.1%
	Married Females	301,722	55.4%	322,459	54.7%	20,737	6.9%
Huntington	Total Males	10,835	100%	11,184	100%	349	3.2%
Station:	Single Males	4,922	45.4%	5,088	45.5%	166	3.4%
	Married Males	5,913	54.6%	6,096	54.5%	183	3.1%
	Total Females	11,647	100%	12,319	100%	672	5.8%
	Single Females	5,635	48.4%	6,224	50.5%	589	10.5%
	Married Females	6,012	51.6%	6,095	49.5%	83	1.4%

Source: 1990 U.S.Census of Population - NYS Data Center, 2000 U.S. Census Table DP-2.

Integral to family structure stability is marital status. In 1990, 59.6 percent of the males living in Suffolk County older than 14 years of age were married while 40.4 percent were single. Similarly, 44.6 percent of women were single with 55.4 percent married. By 2000, males had increased by 1.5 percent, with single males dropping by 5.7 percent and married males growing by 6.5 percent. Single males over 14 now represented 37.5 percent of males, with married males increasing to 62.5 percent. In contrast, by 2000, single females over 14 living in Suffolk County had grown by 10.1 percent, and now represented 45.3 percent of females. Similar to married males, married females grew at a slower 6.9 percent rate, yet decreased to 54.7 percent of Suffolk County females. Between 1990 and 2000, single and married males and females over 14 years of age living in Huntington Station followed a pattern similar to Suffolk County. While Suffolk County males increased by 1.5 percent and females grew by 8.3 percent, Huntington Station males grew by 3.2 percent while females increased by 5.8 percent. However, there were differences in the composition of that growth. Whereas Suffolk County experienced declines in single males and growth in single females over 14, single males and females in Huntington Station both grew between 1990 and 2000. Suffolk County single males decreased by 5.7, with single females increasing 10.1 percent, while single Huntington Station males and females increased by 3.4 and 10.5 percent respectively. In contrast, Suffolk County married males grew by 6.5 percent, with Huntington Station married males increasing by less than half that rate at 3.1 percent. Married Huntington Station females increased slightly by 1.4 percent, almost five times less than the growth rate of Suffolk County married females. While there was evidence of the improvement and strengthening of the Huntington Station family structure, the incidence of marriage still lagged significantly behind that of Suffolk County. In 1990, 45.4 percent of Huntington Station males were single, with 54.6 percent married, while 48.4 percent of females were single and 51.6 percent married. By 2000, reflecting the differing rates of increase in Huntington Station married males and females, 45.5 percent of males were single and 54.5 percent were married, while 50.5 percent of females were single and 49.5 percent were married. By 2000 in Suffolk County, 62.5 percent of males and 54.7 percent of females were married, an increase for males from the 1990 level of 59.6 and a marginal decrease for females from 55.4 percent.

CHAPTER IV
ACADEMIC ACHIEVEMENT:

If a correlation exists between academic achievement and higher family income, as was the case for North Amityville, then those advancing to higher education have an opportunity to work in higher paying jobs. Such a correlation was found between 1990 and 2000, where similarities in patterns of school enrollment and educational achievement between Suffolk County and the Huntington Station community became evident.

Table 4: School Enrollment (3 years of age and older)

		1990		2000		Increase (Decrease)	
Suffolk	Preliminary	28,516	8.2%	31,658	8.2%	3,142	11.0%
County:	Elementary-H.S.	218,985	63.0%	273,741	70.6%	54,756	25.0%
	College	100,187	28.8%	82,092	21.2%	(18,095)	(18.1%)
	Total	347,688	100%	387,491	100%	39,803	11.4%
Huntington	Preliminary	609	8.5%	557	7.4%	(52)	(8.5%)
Station:	Elementary-H.S.	4,379	61.3%	5,473	72.8%	1,094	25.0%
	College	2,157	30.2%	1,485	19.8%	(672)	(31.2%)
	Total	7,145	100%	7,515	100%	370	5.2%

Source: 1990 U.S. Census Table DP-2, 2000 U.S. Census Table DP-2

In 1990, Suffolk County and Huntington Station exhibited similar patterns of school enrollment, with slight differences in the distribution of that enrollment. Of the 347,688 persons over 3 years of age enrolled in Suffolk County schools, 8.2 percent were enrolled in preliminary (pre-elementary) schools, 63 percent were in elementary through high school, and 28.8 percent were attending college. By comparison, of the 7,145 Huntington Station school enrollees, 8.5 percent attended preliminary schools, 61.3 percent were enrolled in elementary through high school, and 30.2 percent were attending college. By 2000, the similar patterns continued between those enrolled in elementary through high school, excepting those attending college. In Suffolk County, of the 387,491 persons attending school, 8.2 percent were in preliminary schools, 70.6 percent were in elementary through high school, and 21.2 percent were attending college. Of the 7,515 students in Huntington Station, 7.4 percent were in preliminary schools, 72.8 percent were enrolled in elementary through high school, and 19.8 percent were attending college. Any distinguishable enrollment distribution disparity became clear by 2000, where 78.8 percent of Suffolk County school enrollees were in elementary through high school, as compared to 80.2 percent in Huntington Station. The result was a higher education enrollment gap, where the 21.2 percent of those in Suffolk County attending college marginally exceeded the 19.8 percent in Huntington Station. This relationship was opposite of 1990, where the 30.2 percent of Huntington Station college enrollments exceeded the 28.8 percent for Suffolk County. The educational enrollment gap had narrowly expanded, explained in part by the fact that those in Huntington Station attending college decreased by 31.2 percent between 1990 and 2000, a decline 58.0 percent greater than the 18.1 percent drop in Suffolk County. The importance of college enrollment for both Suffolk County and Huntington Station residents is that a correlation exists between higher levels of education and greater family income. That Huntington Station's growth in elementary through high school and college enrollment kept pace with Suffolk County, while still lagging behind, would indicate that increased future family incomes could be anticipated in Huntington Station, providing that students remain attached to their community.

Table 5: Educational Attainment - over 25 years of age

		1990		2000		Increase (Decrease)	
Suffolk	8th Grade or less	50,547	5.9%	41,038	4.3%	(9,509)	(18.8%)
County:	9-12 gr. no diploma	101,571	11.9%	89,136	9.5%	(12,435)	(12.2%)
	High School Grad	281,557	32.9%	294,953	31.3%	13,396	4.8%
	College 1-3 yrs.	225,073	26.3%	258,410	27.4%	33,337	14.8%
	College Grad +	196,295	23.0%	258,864	27.5%	62,569	31.9%
	Total	855,043	100%	942,401	100%	87,358	10.2%
Huntington	8th Grade or less	1,324	7.1%	1,579	8.0%	255	19.3%
Station:	9-12 gr. no diploma	2,592	13.8%	2,401	12.1%	(191)	(7.4%)
	High School Grad	5,393	28.8%	5,563	28.1%	170	3.0%
	College 1-3 yrs.	4,767	25.4%	4,732	23.9%	(35)	(.7%)
	College Grad +	4,679	24.9%	5,516	27.9%	837	17.9%
	Total	18,755	100%	19,791	100%	1,036	5.5%

Source: 1990 U.S. Census Table DP-2, 2000 U.S. Census Table DP-2.

By 1990, an educational attainment gap anomaly had developed between Suffolk County and Huntington Station. While 64.7 and 66.4 percent of the respective 1990 Suffolk County and Huntington Station populations had completed some level of schooling, 82.2 percent of those over 25 years of age in Suffolk County had graduated from high school or gone on to higher education as compared to 79.1 percent in Huntington Station. By 2000, while Huntington Station maintained previous educational attainment levels, the population education attainment gap had disappeared. Those who had attained some level of education were now 66.4 and 66.2 percent of the respective Suffolk County and Huntington Station populations. However, the higher education attainment gap for those over 25 years of age had now widened, with 86.2 percent of those in Suffolk County having graduated from high school and gone on to higher education as compared to 79.9 percent in Huntington Station. One explanation for the widening of the gap was that those in Suffolk County over 25 years of age attaining some level of education increased by 10.2 percent between 1990 and 2000, nearly twice the 5.5 percent growth rate in Huntington Station.

The importance of the over 25 years of age higher education attainment gap is that it occurred after changes in the global economy restructured Long Island's job market from jobs requiring a lesser degree of education and skills to jobs requiring a higher level. By 2000, growth in college and post college education attainment for Suffolk County had increased more than 2.7 times that of Huntington Station. A further indication of the higher education gap is that the 34.3 percent of Huntington Station residents in 2000 who attained higher education levels was slightly higher than the 33.4 percent in 1990, and lagged slightly behind the 36.4 percent in greater Suffolk County, which grew from 31.9 percent in 1990. The issue is whether the narrow higher education attainment gap would correlate with a greater proportion of the Huntington Station population having the skills required for employment in higher paying jobs and result in greater family income.

CHAPTER IV
WORKFORCE EMPLOYMENT:

A correlation was found to exist between the higher levels of educational attainment achieved by Suffolk County and Huntington Station residents, and their respective higher workforce employment rates and representation in higher paying jobs. While Huntington Station's educational enrollment, as a percent of its population, was equivalent to that of Suffolk County, Huntington Station's higher educational achievement levels, while less than Suffolk County, still resulted in similar employment rates and greater representation in higher paying jobs for Huntington Station residents. In 1990, the 665,182 Suffolk County persons over 16 years of age in the workforce represented 50.3 percent of the population, as compared to 51.4 percent of Huntington Station's population of 28,247 persons. By 2000, the relationship between workforce representations had remained basically unchanged. Those employed in the Suffolk County economy had fallen to 48.1 percent of the population, as compared to 49.5 percent of Huntington Station residents. Of note is that despite overall workforce employment decreases from 1990, Huntington Station residents experienced a 16 percent growth in government employment, and a significant decrease in self-employed, both exceeding that of Suffolk County.

Table 6: Workforce Employment - over 16 years of age

		1990		2000		Increase (Decrease)	
Suffolk	Private wage and salary	505,869	76.1%	522,597	76.5%	16,728	3.3%
County:	Government	121,969	18.3%	122,849	18.0%	880	.7%
	Self-employed	37,344	5.6%	37,616	5.5%	272	.7%
	Total	665,182	100%	683,062	100%	17,880	2.7%
Huntington	Private wage and salary	11,780	81.1%	11,891	80.3%	111	.9%
Station:	Government	1,938	13.3%	2,249	15.2%	311	16.0%
	Self-employed	815	5.6%	667	4.5%	(148)	(18.2%)
	Total	14,533	100%	14,807	100%	274	1.9%

Source: 1990 U.S. Census Table DP-3, 2000 U.S. Census Table DP-3.

JOB SKILLS:

As presented in Table 7, employment of Suffolk County and Huntington Station workers in 1990 was comparable in most industry sectors, including jobs in the professional, managerial and administrative categories, which tend to require a higher degree of education. Similarly, clerical, service and machine operators jobs, often requiring a lower degree of education, were the other categories employing large percentages Huntington Station and Suffolk County residents.

Table 7: Employment by Industry Sector

Industry Sector	1990 Suffolk County		Huntington Station	
Technician	23,773	3.6%	531	3.7%
Professional	103,133	15.5%	2,394	16.5%
Manager/Administrator	89,432	13.4%	1,722	11.9%
Sales	85,593	12.9%	2,055	14.1%
Clerical	118,926	17.9%	2,222	15.3%
Crafts/Construct/Mechanic	79,624	12.0%	1,779	12.2%
Machine Operators	26,958	4.1%	724	5.0%
Transportation Operators	25,885	3.8%	490	3.4%
Laborers	20,698	3.1%	594	4.1%
Farm/Fishing	8,573	1.3%	165	1.1%
Service	61,415	9.2%	1,498	10.3%
Private Household	1,964	.3%	76	.5%
Protective Service	19,208	2.9%	283	1.9%
Total	665,182	100%	14,533	100%

Source: 1990 Census, Table DP-3, Labor Force Status and Employment Characteristics.

By 2000, the differing levels of educational attainment between Suffolk County and Huntington Station residents had resulted in little recognizable differences in labor force employment. The 2000 Suffolk County labor force employment for those over 16 years old increased by 2.7 percent to 683,062 and now represented 48.1 percent of the Suffolk County population. Huntington Station's labor force, however, fared better. The 14,807 persons in 2000 working represented 49.5 percent of Huntington Station's population, while reflecting a 1.9 percent employment increase from 1990. Additionally, as presented in Table 6, Huntington Station's employed in private wage and salary jobs increased by .9 percent, as compared to Suffolk County's 3.3 percent growth, while government employment increased by 16.0 percent, in contrast to the .7 percent growth in Suffolk County. Entrepreneurs, the backbone of small business and critical to economic growth of any community, differed significantly between Suffolk County and Huntington Station. In Suffolk County, those who were self-employed increased by .7 percent between 1990 and 2000, and now represented 5.5 percent of the workforce. As an example of two workforce sectors heading in different directions, Huntington Station self-employed individuals, already in short supply, decreased by 18.2 percent and represented only 4.5 percent of the workforce. Furthermore, the percent ratio between the Suffolk County and Huntington Station self-employed had increased from 1.00 to 1.00 in 1990 to 1.22 to 1.00 in 2000. The composition of the respective workforces also changed during the 10 years ending with 2000, and appears in Table 7.

Table 7 (cont.): Employment by Industry Sector

Industry Sector	2000 Suffolk County		Huntington Station	
Professional	70,611	10.4%	1,879	12.7%
Finance/Insur/Real Estate	53,510	7.8%	1,182	8.0%
Sales	112,235	16.4%	2,489	16.8%
Clerical/Information	27,290	4.0%	597	4.0%
Mfg/Construct/Mechanics	116,395	17.1%	2,328	15.7%
Public Administration	38,124	5.6%	505	3.4%
Whse/Transport/Utilities	40,393	5.9%	892	6.0%
Farm/Agric/Fish	2,369	.3%	16	.1%
Service	222,135	32.5%	4,919	33.3%
Total	683,062	100%	14,807	100%

Source: 2000 U.S. Census, Table DP-3

Despite the fact that the increase between 1990 and 2000 of the Huntington Station workforce employment over 16 years of age was proportionately smaller than in Suffolk County, there were similarities in the distribution of jobs between the higher paying professional, managerial and administrative, crafts and construction sectors. These jobs tend to require a higher degree of education and skills, areas in which Huntington Station, while lagging behind, still had kept pace with Suffolk County. Suffolk County's professional jobs decreased by 31.5 percent; and managerial and administrative jobs (now included in Finance, Insurance and Real Estate) decreased by 40.1 percent, while manufacturing, crafts, and construction jobs increased by 46.1 percent. By comparison, Huntington Station lost 21.5 percent of its professional jobs; managerial and administrative employment decreased by 31.4 percent and manufacturing, crafts, and construction employment increased by 30.9 percent. In occupations where a lower level of education would be acceptable, such as clerical and service, Suffolk County grew by 38.3 percent, while Huntington Station, in the aggregate, reported 48.3 percent growth. In sales jobs, Suffolk County increased by 31.1 percent, while Huntington Station reported 21.1 percent growth.

Table 8: Employment Status - Male and Female - 16 years of age and older

		1990		2000		Increase (Decrease)	
Suffolk	Males employed	369,116	55.5%	370,585	54.3%	1,469	.4%
County:	Females employed	296,066	44.5%	312,477	45.7%	16,411	5.5%
	Total	665,182	100%	683,062	100%	17,880	2.7%
Huntington	Males employed	8,023	55.2%	8,242	55.7%	219	2.7%
Station:	Females employed	6,510	44.8%	6,565	44.3%	55	.8%
	Total	14,533	100%	14,807	100%	274	1.9%

Source: 1990 U.S. Census Table DP-3, 2000 U.S. Census Tables DP-3.

In 1990, of the 665,182 persons over 16 years of age employed in Suffolk County, 55.5 percent were male and 44.5 percent females, a 1.25 to 1 ratio. For the 14,533 persons over 16 employed in Huntington Station, 55.2 percent were male and 44.8 percent female, a 1.23 to 1 ratio. By 2000, males in the Suffolk County workforce had increased by .4 percent, while falling to 54.3 percent of the employment base. Females, while increasing by 5.5 percent, also improved their labor force participation ratio, with the male to female ratio in the workforce narrowing to 1.19 to 1. In contrast, by 2000, Huntington Station reported a 2.7 percent increase in employed males and an .8 percent increase in employed females. With the labor force participation ratio widening between males and females, from 1.23 in 1990 to 1.26 in 2000, the result was that males and females employed in Huntington Station were respectively 55.7 and 44.3 percent of the labor force. As female-headed families increased regionally, more females proportionally participated in the labor force increase in Suffolk County than in Huntington Station. An important distinction is that females represented a smaller share of the increase in the Huntington Station workforce, while Suffolk County females did not. Additionally, while there was a smaller proportional labor force increase in Huntington Station than in Suffolk County, the male and female composition of the respective workforces, for the most part, remained unchanged.

Despite the fact that the percent increase in Huntington Station's labor force between 1990 and 2000 was 29.7 percent less than Suffolk County's, Huntington Station reported the same degree of unemployment, when comparing those employed to those who are not. The relationship existing between the employment and unemployment status of males and females over 16 years of age was slightly favorable to Suffolk County over Huntington Station.

Table 9: Unemployed Compared to Workforce (a)

		1990		2000		Increase (Decrease)	
Suffolk County:	Total Workforce	698,716	100%	711,026	100%	12,310	1.8%
	Male unemployed	18,461	2.6%	14,668	2.0%	(3,793)	(20.5%)
	Female unemployed	15,073	2.2%	13,296	1.9%	(1,777)	(11.8%)
	Total	33,534	4.8%	27,964	3.9%	(5,570)	(16.6%)
Huntington Station:	Total Workforce	15,300	100%	15,414	100%	114	.7%
	Male unemployed	373	2.4%	285	1.8%	(88)	(23.6%)
	Female unemployed	394	2.6%	322	2.1%	(72)	(18.3%)
	Total	767	5.0%	607	3.9%	(160)	(20.9%)

Source: 1990 U.S. Census Table DP-3, 2000 U.S. Census Table DP-3.
Note (a): Workforce defined as employed plus unemployed.

The 1990 Suffolk County unemployed represented 4.8 percent of the workforce, with unemployed males approximately 2.6 percent of their workforce force and females 2.2 percent. Huntington Station's 5.0 percent unemployment rate was nearly that of Suffolk County's, with unemployed males and females respectively representing 2.4 and 2.6 percent of Huntington Station's unemployed workforce. By 2000, the Suffolk County unemployed decreased to 3.9 percent of the workforce, a 16.6 percent decline, while Huntington Station's unemployment rate fell by almost 21 percent to 3.9 percent. The unemployment status of Suffolk County males and females in 2000 each decreased to nearly 2 percent of their respective employment bases, with unemployed males and females decreasing respectively by 20.5 and 11.8 percent from 1990. In similar fashion, Huntington Station's male unemployed decreased by 23.6 percent, while females decreased by 18.3 percent. Significant is that between 1990 and 2000; Huntington Station's unemployment rate fell 25 percent more than Suffolk County's rate. Also important is that Huntington Station's workforce grew by less than a third of Suffolk County's, and that the male unemployment rate by 2000 was nearly 10 percent less than Suffolk County's male unemployment rate.

A comparison between the employed and unemployed reveals how Huntington Station had fared as compared to Suffolk County. Between 1990 and 2000, the ratio of the 17,880 increase in employment in the Suffolk County economy for those 16 years of age and older, to the decrease of 5,570 in unemployed was 3.21 to 1. While improving from 1990, Huntington Station's gain in employment of 274 resulted in a workforce where 1.71 new persons were employed for every additional one not working. This resulted in the ratio of employed to unemployed in Huntington Station improving between 1990 and 2000 to where it mirrored Suffolk County. In 1990, the Suffolk County ratio was 19.8 persons employed to every person unemployed, with an 18.9 to 1 ratio in Huntington Station. By 2000, the Suffolk County ratio improved to 24.4 to 1, with Huntington Station also increasing to 24.4 to 1. Surrounded by an economically vibrant Suffolk County, Huntington Station had improved, becoming a community with potential for greater economic activity.

FAMILY INCOME:

The socioeconomic infrastructure of Huntington Station had weakened slightly by 2000. Single parent families had increased to 26.3 percent of all Huntington Station families, and families headed by females were almost 3 times as much as families headed by men. Despite the difficulty that single family heads have in balancing their day care needs and employment responsibilities, Huntington Station residents kept pace with Suffolk County in academic attainment and job skills, resulting in a workforce that was capable of accessing the region's higher paying jobs. However, there were economic consequences of having more women heading families than men. In 2000, women working full time had a median income of $32,935, 24 percent lower than the $43,349[38] earned by their male counterparts. The result is that women family heads often earned less, despite having the requisite skills for higher paying jobs. With these lower wages impacting a greater proportion of single parent families, including Huntington Station families, it is reasonable to conclude that Huntington Station family income would be less than the surrounding Suffolk County. Tables 10 and 11 reflect how family income in Huntington Station, while improving between 1990 and 2000, still lagged behind family income growth for Suffolk County.

---

[38] 2000 U.S. Census Table DP-3, Profile of Selected Economic Characteristics.

Table 10: Nominal Family Income

1990

Nominal Family Income	Suffolk County Families		Huntington Station Families	
$0 - $5,000	4,730	1.4%	254	3.4%
$5,000-$9,999	6,407	1.9%	141	1.9%
$10,000-$14,999	10,536	3.1%	268	3.6%
$15,000-$24,999	27,903	8.1%	688	9.3%
$25,000-$49,999	105,383	30.6%	2,333	31.5%
$50,000-$99,999	147,114	42.8%	3,006	40.6%
Over $100,000	41,538	12.1%	717	9.7%
Total	343,611	100%	7,407	100%

2000

Nominal Family Income	Suffolk County Families		Huntington Station Families	
$0-$9,999	8,561	2.4%	264	3.6%
$10,000-$14,999	6,936	1.9%	234	3.2%
$15,000-$24,999	19,237	5.3%	478	6.7%
$25,000-$49,999	71,600	19.7%	1,516	20.9%
$50,000-$99,999	150,808	41.6%	2,990	41.3%
Over $100,000	105,715	29.1%	1,760	24.3%
Total	362,857	100%	7,242	100%

Source: 1990 U.S. Census Table DP-4, Income and Poverty Status in 1989; 2000 U.S. Census Table DP-3, Profile of Selected Economic Characteristics: 2000.

In 1990, the 8.9 percent of Huntington Station families earning below $15,000 exceeded the 6.4 percent of Suffolk County families earning $15,000 or less. Fewer Huntington Station families also earned over $25,000, with 85.5 percent of Suffolk County families earning in excess of $25,000, as compared to 81.8 percent for Huntington Station families. Furthermore, 50.3 percent of Huntington Station families earned over $50,000, as compared with 54.9 percent of Suffolk County families. By 2000, correlating with improving educational attainment, economic conditions improved to where only 4.3 percent of Suffolk County families and 6.8 percent of Huntington Station families were earning below $15,000, and 90.4 percent of Suffolk County families earned more than $25,000, followed by 86.5 percent of Huntington Station families. In part because more residents attended or graduated from college, Suffolk County families earning over $50,000 improved from 54.9 percent in 1990 to 70.7 percent in 2000. Furthermore, the gap between families earning over $100,000 annually had also narrowed. In 1990, the 12.1 percent rate of Suffolk County families earning over $100,000 was 25 percent greater than the 9.7 percent of Huntington Station families. By 2000, Suffolk County families earning over $100,000 more than doubled to 29.1 percent, and were now only 20 percent more than Huntington Station, a drop of 20 percent from 1990. In Huntington Station, 24.3 percent of the families now earned over $100,000, nearly a three-fold increase from 1990. Reflecting similar percents of college attendees and graduates, Huntington Station families earning over $50,000 per year, while improving from 50.3 percent in 1990 to 65.6 percent by 2000, not only still lagged behind Suffolk County, but the gap had widened by 10.7 percent.

Mean per capita and family median income variances also existed between Suffolk County and Huntington Station, and are presented in Table 11.

Table 11: Mean Per Capita and Median Family (Nominal and Real) Income

		1990		2000	
		Mean Per Capita	**Median Family**	**Mean Per Capita**	**Median Family**
Suffolk	Nominal $	$18,481	$53,247	$26,577	$72,112
County:	Real $ (1)	$13,392	$38,585	$14,603	$39,622
Huntington	Nominal $	$17,870	$50,184	$23,689	$67,115
Station:	Real $ (1)	$12,949	$36,365	$13,016	$36,876

Source: 1990 U.S. Census Table DP-4, 2000 U.S. Census Table DP-3.
Note (1): Adjusted for Inflation; Based on 1984 CPI as the base year, New York Area Index as of July 1990 and July 2000.

The 1990 Huntington Station mean per capita and median family income, as expressed in both nominal and real dollars, were respectively 97 and 94 percent of their Suffolk County equivalent. By 2000, however, this gap had widened. The Suffolk County nominal mean per capita and median family incomes experienced a respective 44 and 35 percent growth between 1990 and 2000, while mean per capita and median family income expressed in real dollars grew by 9.0 and 2.7 percent respectively. The growth of Huntington Station's mean per capita and median family income expressed in nominal dollars lagged behind at 33 and 34 percent, with mean per capita and median family income expressed in real dollars also lagging behind, with marginal increases of .5 and 1.4 percent respectively. The Huntington Station mean per capita and median family income expressed in both nominal and real dollars had now fallen to 89 and 93 percent of their Suffolk County equivalents. Not only had Huntington Station failed to keep pace with Suffolk County, but actually lost economic ground.

HOUSING:

As would be expected, with the additional costs of home ownership, including down payment requirements, the lower mean per capita and median family incomes in Huntington Station impacted the incidence of home ownership, as reflected in Table 12.

Table 12: Occupied Housing Units

		1990		2000		Increase (Decrease)	
Suffolk County:	Total occupied units	424,719	100%	469,299	100%	44,580	10.5%
	Owner occupied	340,253	80.1%	374,360	79.8%	34,107	10.0%
	Renter occupied	84,466	19.9%	94,939	20.2%	10,473	12.4%
	Persons/Owner Occup.	3.16		3.07		(.09)	(2.8%)
	Persons/Renter Occup.	2.57		2.55		(.02)	(.8%)
Huntington Station:	Total occupied units	9,591	100%	9,731	100%	140	1.5%
	Owner occupied	6,643	69.3%	6,830	70.2%	187	2.8%
	Renter occupied	2,948	30.7%	2,901	29.8%	(47)	(1.6%)
	Persons/Owner Occup.	3.01		3.00		(.01)	(.3%)
	Persons/Renter Occup.	2.74		3.19		.45	16.4%

Source: 1990 U.S. Census Table DP-1, 2000 U.S. Census Tables DP-1.

In 1990, of the total occupied housing units in Suffolk County, 80.1 percent were owner occupied and 19.9 percent renter occupied. Of Huntington Station's total occupied housing units, 69.3 percent were owner occupied with 30.7 percent renter occupied. By 2000, total Suffolk County housing units had increased by 10.5 percent, with 77 percent of the increase owner occupied units, and 23 percent renter occupied. In Huntington Station, the total occupied housing units increased by 1.5 percent, with 133 percent of the increase owner occupied units, netted against a 33 percent decrease in renter occupied units. While Suffolk County experienced a more balanced 10.0 and 12.4 percent respective increase in owner and renter occupied housing units, Huntington Station reported owner occupied unit growth of 2.8 percent, and a renter occupied housing unit decrease of 1.6 percent. Suffolk County's growth rate in owner occupied housing units had lagged slightly behind that of renter occupied units, while the opposite was occurring in Huntington Station, where the owner occupied housing unit growth rate increased nearly four times faster than the rate for renter occupied units.

Not only had housing unit growth in Huntington Station lagged behind Suffolk County, that housing had become more crowded. In Suffolk County, which reported 7.4 percent growth in population between 1990 and 2000, persons per owner occupied and renter occupied units decreased, primarily due to the 10.5 percent increase in total housing units. By comparison, Huntington Station's population increased by 5.9 percent, while total occupied units increased by only 1.5 percent, resulting in more crowded housing. Persons per owner occupied units remained basically unchanged, marginally decreasing by .3 percent, while persons per rental housing units increased significantly by 16.4 percent, from 2.74 persons in 1990 to 3.19 persons in 2000.

In a trend that continued between 1990 and 2000, the 1990 median gross rent in Huntington Station of $658 was 5.5 percent less than the Suffolk County median gross rent of $696. By 2000, the median gross rent of Huntington Station had increased 41 percent to $927, as compared to the 36 percent increase in Suffolk County's median gross rent to $945 (1990 U.S. Census, table DP-1, 2000 U.S. Census table DP-4). Despite lower family incomes, renters in Huntington Station not only continued to pay almost as much rent as Suffolk County as a whole, but that gross rent was now only 1.9 percent lower than the median gross rent of Suffolk County, significantly narrowing the gap from 1990.

CHAPTER IV
SUMMARY:

As compared to Suffolk County, Huntington Station began in 1990 from a slightly less favorable position in the areas of family structure and academic attainment, workforce participation, job distribution, household income, and home ownership. In particular, during the 10 year period covered by this research, in comparison to the surrounding Suffolk County, Huntington Station:

(1) Despite having a population growth rate slightly below that of Suffolk County, Huntington Stations black community decreased with Hispanics and others growing a a rate disproportionate to the Suffolk County Hispanic and Asian growth rate;

(2) Experienced a decrease in families with a male and female present, and had more families headed by women than men;

(3) Had a weakening of traditional family structure, where single males and females grew at a faster rate than married males and females;

(4) Had greater negative growth in college enrollments than Suffolk County, with equivalent student enrollment growth in elementary and high school;

(5) Had significantly slower growth in post-secondary education attainment;

(6) Had a significant decrease in self-employed entrepreneurs, a marginal increase in private sector employment, and a significant increase in government employment;

(7) Had comparable distribution in higher paying professional, craft, construction, and machine operator jobs, and similar increases in lower paying service, clerical, and sales jobs;

(8) Experienced slight growth in workforce employment, with steeper decreases in both male and female unemployment;

(9) Had growth comparable to Suffolk County in both nominal median family and nominal mean per capita income, with nearly half of Huntington Station families earning nominal median income above $67,115, as compared to Suffolk County where a just less than half of the families earned below the nominal median income of $72,112;

(10) Had real mean per capita and real median real family income growing at a slower rate than Suffolk County's, with a marginal increase in Huntington Station's real mean per capita income;

(11) Had a slightly higher owner occupied housing units and a marginal decrease in renter occupied units, while Suffolk County reported significant growth for both.

Overall, despite experiencing growth in the socioeconomic indicators between 1990 and 2000, Huntington Station, while keeping pace with surrounding Suffolk County, continued to lag behind. What then can Huntington Station do to adapt to the changes imposed by the global economy. The following analysis builds on the untapped potential of Huntington Station in returning it to its cultural and economic roots as an important Suffolk County downtown.

Huntington Station: A Path for Economic Growth

Economic development is incremental and depends heavily on people. Bricks and mortar can rebuild a business district and community, but it is the talent of people that makes that development lasting. The presented socioeconomic profile of Huntington Station, while slightly weaker than Suffolk County, provides instances where opportunities for economic growth in a global economy are possible. The foundation is there, since Huntington Station was once a vibrant part of Suffolk County's economic base.

With this in mind, any economic development plan for the Huntington Station community and business district must be designed to take advantage of the competitive advantages of the community. Those identified socioeconomic workforce weaknesses that can be built upon are:

(1) **An untapped entrepreneurial class** that decreased by 18.2 percent between 1990 and 2000. By 2000, the percentage of Huntington Station entrepreneurs, as part of the Huntington Station workforce, had now fallen to 81.8% of the percentage of Suffolk County's entrepreneurs in the Suffolk County workforce; a significant decrease from 1990, when the percentage of entrepreneurs in the Huntington Station workforce equaled that of Suffolk County. This would indicate that there is growth potential in Huntington Station's entrepreneurial class, as every community often has untapped entrepreneurs, each representing a potential business. Experience indicates that many entrepreneurs begin by operating out of a home, garage, or a single building, dispersed, uncentered, disconnected and unrooted. Providing incentives that not only encourage cultivation of Huntington Station's entrepreneurs, but also concentrate their economic activity in the Huntington Station business district, will provide an important economic spark that can contribute to revitalizing any new contemplated downtown. By attracting entrepreneurs to Huntington Station's central business district, storefronts will become occupied, vacant land built upon, and dilapidated buildings rehabilitated.

(2) **A local workforce with improved earnings potential**. Huntington Station's workforce is burdened with a family structure where single males or females head 26.3 percent of all Huntington Station families with children under 18. Furthermore, single-family heads are a greater percentage of total Huntington Station families than their Suffolk County counterparts. Huntington Station's weaker family structure is the result of a decade where families with both a male and female present decreased, resulting in more families headed by women than men. This is important because single-family heads not only have income earning responsibilities, but have child-care concerns as well. With higher educational attainment levels, the Huntington Station workforce is well suited to access the local jobs created by the global economy. Providing daycare support will allow single family heads to either seek higher paying jobs, or become employed, thereby increasing Huntington Station's combined workforce employment rate and household income.

(3) **The lower median family income** and mean per capita income in Huntington Station, as compared to Suffolk County, continues a decade long erosion in Huntington Station's mean per capita income. The loss of economic ground, while not steep, was caused by the slower adaptation of Huntington Station's workforce to Long Island's changing job market, caused in part by the globalization of the world's economy and the impact of that change on the Long Island economy. Contributing to the lower median family income are the combination of more female family heads who traditionally earn lower

salaries than their male counterparts, and the Huntington Station workforce's comparatively lower educational attainment levels, which often make it more difficult to access the region's higher paying jobs currently created by the global marketplace. This situation can be improved with a coordinated policy that addresses aspects of entrepreneurial development, job training and workforce support.

We now have some perspective as to how the global economy and deindustrialization of the Long Island economy affected Suffolk County and two communities of color, North Amityville and Huntington Station. Would the same results occur in Nassau County, and in particular the primarily black community of Roosevelt? Andreaus Guilty, a long time Roosevelt resident tells of his recollections in the following analysis of Roosevelt: An Untapped Economic Resource.

Chapter V

ROOSEVELT COMMUNITY:
AN UNTAPPED ECONOMIC RESOURCE

The primarily African-American community of Roosevelt experienced socioeconomic changes between 1990 and 2000. Roosevelt has remained segregated, while experiencing growth in the Asian and Pacific Islander populations. Several indices point to Roosevelt's economic struggles; as compared to the economic development that has characterized Nassau County. There has been a decrease in married households, with single headed households increasing dramatically to where they represent nearly 1 in 2 families, more than two and a half the rate of Nassau County. While the educational enrollment in advanced grades are somewhat comparable to Nassau County, overall educational attainment levels are much lower in Roosevelt, and in part explain the larger decrease in Roosevelt employment levels as compared to Nassau County. The Roosevelt unemployment rates were higher, and labor participation rates were lower, than surrounding Nassau County, with the Roosevelt workforce more widely employed in jobs requiring fewer skills than the greater Nassau County. Moreover, fewer Roosevelt residents owned their own homes, while more were living in rental apartments, paying comparable high rents.

Observing the changes was Andreaus Guilty, who was born in 1964 into a family that eventually grew to include five brothers and sisters. His mother, a nurse, emigrated from Kentucky to Roosevelt's adjoining community of Freeport during the 1960's. During that time she met his father, a blue-collar machine shop operator manufacturing dye molds for plastics.[39] Long Island was then, and continues today to be the largest concentration of machine shops in New York State.

When Andreaus's parents married they settled in the family home they purchased in the nearby Liberty Park area of Freeport, in the Town of Hempstead and the County of Nassau. Hempstead Town is the largest populated town in the United States. The family lived in that home until the urban renewal program of the 1970's tore down the house along with others in the Liberty Park neighborhood. After that Andreaus's parents went their separate ways living in rental apartments, his father in Freeport and his mother in Roosevelt. Shortly thereafter his parents divorced, and Andreaus, age 14, and his brothers and sisters lived with his mother on Centennial Avenue in Roosevelt.[40]

Andreaus recalls that his early years were a black Norman Rockwell experience. While he recalls the demonstrations of the civil rights movement in the 1960's he was too young to participate in them. Despite being forced by his mother to attend church, he enjoyed growing up during the 1960's and early 1970's, having fun bicycling on the community bike path, trick-or-treating during Halloween, and spending a lot of recreational time in the park on the swings and other park amenities. His experience in high school was a good one. He was the class clown, had good grades, and better ones when he tried.[41]

After high school he was admitted to Hofstra University under the New Opportunities at Hofstra Program that provided a four-year scholarship to disadvantaged children. During that time however, Andreaus became involved with black awareness through the

---

[39] Andreaus Guilty, Personal Interview. 31 May 2006.
[40] Ibid.
[41] Ibid.

hip-hop group Spectrum City and only completed one semester at Hofstra. Andreaus felt that the program had too much structure and too much control over him. He recalls that he had become too black for the program, and it was feared that his non-conformist ways would sow the seeds of discontent on campus. He decided to leave Hofstra and pursue a music career; following in the path of the many groups that he had seen perform in Roosevelt.[42]

As a teenager during the 1970's Andreaus grew up in the center of black entrepreneurism on Nassau Road in Roosevelt, that also was the commercial center of the community. To Andreaus it seemed that black entrepreneurs owned everything. There was a supermarket, movie theatre, pool halls, bars, taxis, gas stations, black falcons motorcycle club, small black owned businesses, and a roller rink where the beginning of hip-hop in Roosevelt emerged. Roosevelt had become rich in culture and talent and attracted to the roller rink performing groups such as BB King, Run DMC, Curtis Blow, and Funky Four Plus 1. At another venue, Mr. Hicks Place, comedian Eddie Murphy first appeared.[43]

The atmosphere in Roosevelt began to change during the 1980's, with the beginning of the Town of Hempstead urban renewal programs coinciding with the weakening of the local economy. The movie theater burned down and was not allowed to rebuild. The roller rink, which was owned by four black entrepreneurs was taken over for failure to pay taxes and has now been replaced by housing. Western Beef and a thrift shop replaced the supermarket. Gentrification occurred and all the black businesses on the strip shopping center disappeared. At the same time Andreaus began to experience discrimination, primarily based on the community being stripped of its economic assets resulting from the urban renewal programs, and the limited funding of community programs by Nassau County and the Town of Hempstead. Economic activity that had once benefited local entrepreneurs and the Roosevelt community had now been replaced by entrepreneurs living outside of the community, effectively exporting local dollars and weakening the economic structure of Roosevelt.[44]

The 1980's were also important to Andreaus's emergence as a hip-hop entertainer through two career-altering experiences. The first was a Rick James concert at the Nassau Veterans Memorial Coliseum attended by Andreaus who, after watching Rick James concluded that he could do the same performing. Andreaus began saving money and purchased musical equipment and performed at parties until he earned the money necessary to create a record. The second experience was the evolution of the hip-hop pioneering group Public Enemy from Spectrum City, a group with whom Andreaus already had a relationship. Public Enemy members Chuck D, Hank Shockley, Flavor Flave and Bill Stephaney liked Andreaus's work, and produced songs performed by him on their records under the name Andreaus 13, a name that he prefers, and is still known by. The relationship between Andreaus 13 and Public Enemy lasted from 1988 to 1993 with Public Enemy producing and releasing his records.[45]

Andreaus 13 continued to live with his brothers and sisters at his mother's home until 1988 when he got married at 24 years of age. He has 6 children from relationships with two women one of whom he married and later divorced. He met his wife while at Roosevelt High School. The two eldest children are in their 20's and are pursuing their own careers, the other four are living with their mother, to whom Andreaus pays child sup-

[42] Ibid.
[43] Ibid.
[44] Ibid.
[45] Ibid.

port. Today, Andreaus owns his own home in nearby Uniondale, his mother has retired to a senior citizen community in the Town of Hempstead, and his brothers and sisters live in communities from North Carolina to Long Island.[46]

Since 1993 Andreaus 13 has owned and operated the African-American Media Network. That is where I first met Andreaus 13. In my role as project director of the Long Island Neighborhood Development Initiative (LINDI) I visited his studio to see what LINDI could do to help him. The studio was in his apartment on the top floor of a three-floor walk-up building, and was fashioned from a large closet with a camera, metal foil and floodlights. It was hard not to see Andreaus 13's potential. He had moxie, and the smarts, passion and perseverance to see his vision succeed. What he has accomplished since that first meeting testifies to that.

He no longer operates his studio from his apartment, nor does he continue to live there. He owns and operates a public access television show covering black news, a television production studio, and a music-recording studio. He also participates in career programs mentoring local school children about the music industry. He lives in a home he purchased in Uniondale Long Island, and his production studios are now located in very comfortable commercial spaces just off Nassau Road, the main commercial corridor of Roosevelt.

What drives Andreaus 13 are his beliefs that music today has to be positive and responsible. His frustration is that today's music is to geared to contemporary interests such as violence, sex, sensationalism, and race; the kind of music that he calls not uplifting. The original hip-hop that he was a part of had poetry, words, a beat, a melody, and was produced for DJ's and dancers.[47] The African-American Media Network studios are contributing to a better Roosevelt by creating an environment that discovers and nurtures talent by providing an outlet for that talent. The facility is also where former rap artists can perform.

Andreaus 13 is also concerned about Roosevelt's micro-economic activity. For that to grow he believes that there has to be a comfort level established for the intellectually sound belief that a black business can be profitable. That will attract capital to the community. He also believes that African Americans have an unmet need for news reporting tailored to their community.[48]

Institutional racism, or the heavy burden blacks must carry, or the obstacles that must be overcome in order to get ownership to projects in the Roosevelt community concerns Andreaus 13, because of how it prevents economic growth of the Roosevelt economy. Ownership builds wealth, and for the Roosevelt community to grow economically it must share in that wealth. Andreaus 13 has experienced institutional racism in his efforts to expand his media center so it can become an African-American news channel. He believes that a market exists, especially since the purchase of Black Entertainment Network resulted in the disappearance of the black news segments. However, with corporations apparently not interested in black news and without a national news outlet for black people, Andreaus 13's goal is to access that market. He calls the lack of quality of Black news the dumbing down of black America through institutional racism.[49]

Andreaus Guilty has spent his entire life of 42 years in the Town of Hempstead community of Roosevelt, bearing witness to the decline of the quality of life, erosion of the local economy, and the disappearance of black entrepreneurs. Quantifying Roosevelt's

[46] Ibid.
[47] Ibid.
[48] Ibid.
[49] Ibid.

CHAPTER V

experience in adjusting to the global economy appears below in an analysis of a broad range of social indicators and economic data reflecting how Roosevelt, a depressed economic community, did not fare as well as Nassau County.

ROOSEVELT: THE SOCIO-ECONOMIC FABRIC OF A COMMUNITY

POPULATION:
Table 1: Racial Composition

		1990		2000		Increase (Decrease)	
Nassau	Total	1,287,348	100%	1,334,544	100%	47,196	3.7%
County:	White	1,115,119	86.6%	1,058,285	79.3%	(56,834)	(5.1%)
	Black	111,057	8.6%	134,673	10.1%	23,616	21.3%
	Other(a)	61,172	4.8%	141,586	10.6%	80,414	131.5%
Roosevelt:	Total	15,030	100%	15,854	100%	824	5.5%
	White	1,185	7.9%	1,263	8.0%	78	6.6%
	Black	13,331	88.7%	12,528	79.0%	(803)	(6.0%)
	Other	514	3.4%	2,063	13.0%	1,549	301.4%

Source: 1990 U.S. Census, Table DP-1. 2000 U. S. Census, Table DP-1.
Note (a): Other includes Natural Americans, Asians and Pacific Islanders.

The total Nassau County population grew by 3.7 percent between 1990 and 2000, to a total of 1,334,544, whereas by 2000, the Roosevelt community reported growth of 5.5 percent to 15,854. While the population growth percentages were similar, the changes in their racial composition were not. In 1990, whites and blacks respectively represented 86.6 and 8.6 percent of Nassau County's population. By 2000 the black component of Nassau County's population had increased to 10.1 percent, while whites decreased to 79.3 percent; the non-white non-black population (termed other) rose from 4.8 percent to 10.6 percent. Blacks grew at a faster pace; increasing by 21.3 percent or 23,616 persons to 134,673, while Whites decreasing by 56,834 people, fell by 5.1 percent.

Between 1990 and 2000, while the total population of Roosevelt increased, the concentration of blacks residents did not. In 1990, the Roosevelt population was 7.9 percent white and 88.7 percent black. By 2000, the Roosevelt population of 15,854 represented growth of 5.5 percent, with whites and other accounting for all the growth. The white population had increased by 6.6 percent, with those remaining representing only 8 percent of the Roosevelt population. Others, including Asian and Pacific Islanders, however, increasing by 301.4 percent to 2,063 persons, now represented 13 percent of the population. Blacks, while decreasing 6.0 percent to 12,528, were 79.0 percent of Roosevelt's population, making the concentrated black community of Roosevelt more segregated than the rest of Nassau County. In contrast, while Nassau County as a whole appeared slightly more integrated, Roosevelt and other Long Island communities where black majorities existed, such as North Amityville, Hempstead Village, and North Bellport, actually became more segregated.

FAMILY STRUCTURE:
Table 2: Family Composition (with children under 18 years of age)

		1990		2000		Increase (Decrease)	
Nassau	Total Families	344,502	100%	347,026	100%	2,524	.7%
County:	Husband/Wife	286,638	83.2%	282,126	81.3%	(4,512)	(1.6%)
	Male head	13,914	4.0%	15,958	4.6%	2,044	14.7%
	Female head	43,950	12.8%	48,942	14.1%	4,992	11.4%
	Persons per family	2.94		3.34		.4	13.6%
Roosevelt:	Total Families	3,204	100%	3,361	100%	157	4.9%
	Husband/Wife	1,889	59.0%	1,795	53.4%	(94)	(5.0%)
	Male head	251	7.8%	335	10.0%	84	33.5%
	Female head	1,064	33.2%	1,231	36.6%	167	15.7%
	Persons per family	3.90		3.98		.08	2.1%

Source: 1990 U.S. Census Table DP-1, 2000 Census Table DP-1.

Changes in family composition between 1990 and 2000 reflected greater structural weakening of the two-parent household in both Roosevelt, and the surrounding Nassau County. As shown in Table 2, single parent families rose 49.2 percent in Roosevelt, nearly twice the 26.1 percent growth rate in Nassau County. However, as an example of two communities heading in somewhat the same direction, is that between 1990 and 2000 two-parent families with children under 18 decreased by 5 percent in Roosevelt and by 1.6 percent for Nassau County as a whole. By 2000, 18.7 percent of families with children in the greater Nassau County had single parent households, compared to 16.8 percent one decade earlier. In Roosevelt, 1990 single-family households were already at a high level of 41 percent of all households, growing 46.6 percent by 2000.

In contrast to the 2000 family structure in Nassau County where 85.9 percent of families with children less than 18 years of age had a male present, a male presence was reported in only 63.4 percent of Roosevelt families. Both represented a decrease from 1990, where 87.2 percent of Nassau County families had a male present as compared to 66.8 percent of Roosevelt families. The average 1990 Roosevelt family size of 3.9 persons was in excess of 30 percent more crowded than the 2.94 persons in the average Nassau County family. However, by 2000, family demographics had changed. Families in Roosevelt with a husband and wife had decreased by 5 percent, male headed families increased by 33.5 percent, and families headed by females increased by 15.7 percent. While families with children under 18 in Nassau County experienced only a .7 percent growth between 1990 and 2000, families in Roosevelt increased by a 4.9 percent to 3,361. While there was little growth in total Nassau County families, the average 2000 family became larger, increasing by 13.6 percent from 1990 to 3.34 persons per family. Despite families in Roosevelt growing by 4.9 percent, they became slightly more crowded, growing by 2.1 percent to 3.98 persons.

Table 3: Marital Status (those 14 years of age and older)

		1990		2000		Increase (Decrease)	
Nassau County:	Total Males	501,794	100%	469,049	100%	(32,745)	(6.5%)
	Single Males	202,633	40.4%	173,390	37.0%	(29,243)	(14.4%)
	Married Males	299,161	59.6%	295,659	63.0%	(3,502)	(1.2%)
	Total Females	553,856	100%	589,567	100%	35,711	6.4%
	Single Females	255,156	46.1%	257,499	43.7%	2,343	.9%
	Married Females	298,700	53.9%	332,068	56.3%	33,368	11.2%
Roosevelt:	Total Males	5,326	100%	5,160	100%	(166)	(3.1%)
	Single Males	3,219	60.4%	2,973	57.6%	(246)	(7.6%)
	Married Males	2,107	39.6%	2,187	42.4%	80	3.8%
	Total Females	6,194	100%	6,626	100%	432	7.0%
	Single Females	4,237	68.4%	4,038	60.9%	(199)	(4.7%)
	Married Females	1,957	31.6%	2,588	39.1%	631	32.2%

Source:1990 U.S.Census of Population-NYS Data Center, 2000 U.S. Census Table DP-2.

Integral to family structure stability is the marital status of men and women. In 1990, 59.6 percent of the males living in Nassau County older than 14 years of age were married while 40.4 percent were single. Similarly, 46.1 percent of women were single with 53.9 percent married. By 2000, males had decreased by 6.5 percent, with single males dropping by 14.4 percent and married males falling at a slower 1.2 percent rate. Single males over 14 now represented 37 percent of males, with married males increasing to 63 percent. In similar fashion, by 2000, single females over 14 living in Nassau County had marginally increased by .9 percent, and now represented 43.7 percent of females. In contrast, married females growing by a much faster 11.2 percent rate, increased to 56.3 percent of Nassau County females.

Between 1990 and 2000, single and married males and females over 14 years of age living in Roosevelt followed a pattern similar to Nassau County. While Nassau County males decreased by 6.5 percent and females grew by 6.4 percent, Roosevelt males fell by 3.1 percent and females increased by 7.0 percent. However, there were differences in the composition of that growth. Whereas Nassau County experienced declines in single males and slight growth in females over 14, single males and females in Roosevelt declined at a slower pace between 1990 and 2000. Nassau County single males decreased by 14.4, with females increasing .9 percent, while single Roosevelt males and females decreased by 7.6 and 4.7 percent respectively. In dramatic contrast, Nassau County married males fell by 1.2 percent as Roosevelt married males increased by 3.8 percent, whereas married Roosevelt females increased by 32.2 percent, exceeding the 11.2 percent growth of Nassau County married females. While there was evidence of the improvement and strengthening of the Roosevelt family structure, the incidence of marriage still lagged significantly behind that of Nassau County. In 1990, 60.4 percent of Roosevelt males were single, with 39.6 percent married, while 68.4 percent of females were single and 31.6 percent married. By 2000, reflecting the increase in Roosevelt married males and females, of the males, 57.6 percent were single and 42.4 percent were married, while 60.9 percent of females were single and 39.1 percent were married. By 2000 in Nassau County, 63 percent of males and 56.3 percent of females were married, increasing from 1990 levels of 59.6 and 53.9 percent respectively.

ACADEMIC ACHIEVEMENT:

If a correlation exists between academic achievement and higher family income, it may therefore be reasoned that those advancing to higher education have an opportunity to work in higher paying jobs. Such a correlation developed between 1990 and 2000, where differences in the pattern of school enrollment and in educational achievement between Nassau County and the Roosevelt community emerged.

Table 4: School Enrollment (3 years of age and older)

		1990		2000		Increase (Decrease)	
Nassau	Preliminary	27,741	8.8%	30,116	8.4%	2,375	8.6%
County:	Elementary-H.S.	187,696	59.0%	246,184	68.8%	58,488	31.2%
	College	102,438	32.2%	81,375	22.8%	(21,063)	(20.6%)
	Total	317,875	100%	357,675	100%	39,800	12.5%
Roosevelt:	Preliminary	280	6.4%	365	7.1%	85	30.4%
	Elementary-H.S.	2,917	66.4%	3,734	73.2%	817	28.0%
	College	1,192	27.2%	1,005	19.7%	(187)	(15.7%)
	Total	4,389	100%	5,104	100%	715	16.3%

Source: 1990 U.S. Census Table DP-2, 2000 U.S. Census Table DP-2.

In 1990, while Nassau County and Roosevelt exhibited similar patterns of school enrollment, there were discernible differences in the distribution of that enrollment. Of the 317,875 persons over 3 years of age enrolled in Nassau County schools, 8.8 percent were enrolled in preliminary schools, 59 percent were in elementary through high school, and 32.2 percent were attending college. By comparison, of the 4,389 Roosevelt school enrollees, 6.4 percent attended preliminary schools, 66.4 percent were enrolled in elementary through high school, and 27.2 percent were attending college. By 2000, the differing patterns narrowed between those enrolled in elementary through high school and those attending college. In Nassau County, of the 357,675 persons attending school, 8.4 percent were in preliminary schools, 68.8 percent were in elementary through high school, and 22.8 percent were attending college. Of the 5,104 students in Roosevelt, 7.1 percent were in preliminary schools, 73.2 percent were enrolled in elementary through high school, and 19.7 percent were attending college. The enrollment distribution disparity became less clear by 2000, where 91.6 percent of Nassau County school attendees were in elementary through high school or more, as compared to 92.9 percent in Roosevelt. The result was a narrowing higher education enrollment gap, where the 22.8 percent of those in Nassau County attending college marginally exceeded the 19.7 percent in Roosevelt. The educational enrollment gap had narrowed, explained in part by the fact that those in Roosevelt attending college decreased by 15.7 percent between 1990 and 2000, a slower percentage decline than the 20.6 percent drop in Nassau County. The importance of college enrollment for both Nassau County and Roosevelt residents is that a correlation exists between higher levels of education and greater household income. That Roosevelt's growth in elementary through high school and college enrollment kept pace with Nassau County, while still lagging behind, would indicate that increased future household incomes could be anticipated in Roosevelt, providing that students remain attached to their community.

Table 5: Educational Attainment - over 25 years of age

		1990		2000		Increase (Decrease)	
Nassau County:	8th Grade or less	52,599	6.0%	47,776	5.2%	(4,823)	(9.2%)
	9-12 gr. no diploma	86,546	9.8%	72,962	8.0%	(13,584)	(15.7%)
	High School Grad	266,264	30.2%	243,454	26.8%	(22,810)	(8.6%)
	College 1-3 yrs.	211,557	24.0%	223,180	24.6%	11,623	5.5%
	College Grad +	264,071	30.0%	321,321	35.4%	57,250	21.7%
	Total	881,037	100%	908,693	100%	27,656	3.1%
Roosevelt:	8th Grade or less	736	8.2%	1,194	12.6%	458	62.2%
	9-12 gr. no diploma	1,772	19.9%	1,593	16.8%	(179)	(10.1%)
	High School Grad.	2,824	31.7%	2,914	30.8%	90	3.2%
	College 1-3 yrs.	2,443	27.4%	2,413	25.5%	(30)	(1.2%)
	College Grad +	1,147	12.8%	1,357	14.3%	210	18.3%
	Total	8,922	100%	9,471	100%	549	6.2%

Source: 1990 U.S. Census Table DP-2, 2000 U.S. Census Table DP-2.

By 1990, an educational attainment gap had developed between Nassau County and Roosevelt. While 68.4 and 59.4 percent of the respective 1990 Nassau County and Roosevelt populations had completed some level of schooling, 84.2 percent of those over 25 years of age in Nassau County had graduated high school or gone on to higher education as compared to 71.9 percent in Roosevelt. By 2000, while Roosevelt maintained educational attainment levels, the education attainment gap had grown by 3.9 percent. Those over 25 years of age having attained some level of education had grown to 68.1 and 59.7 percent of the respective Nassau County and Roosevelt populations, with 86.8 percent of those in Nassau County having graduated high school and gone on to higher education as compared to 70.6 percent in Roosevelt. While the educational attainment gap had widened, those in Nassau County over 25 years of age attending school increased by 3.1 percent between 1990 and 2000, lagging behind the 6.2 percent growth in Roosevelt.

The importance of this education attainment gap is that it occurred after changes in the global economy restructured the job market from jobs requiring a lesser degree of education and skills to jobs requiring a higher level. While there was comparable growth in college and post college education attainment, the 23.8 percent of Roosevelt residents attaining higher education levels still lagged behind the 40.8 percent in greater Nassau County, drawing the correlation that a greater proportion of the Roosevelt population was employed in lower paying jobs, resulting in lower family income.

WORKFORCE EMPLOYMENT:

A correlation was found to exist between the higher levels of educational attainment levels achieved by Nassau County residents, their higher workforce employment rates, and their greater representation in higher paying jobs. While Roosevelt's percent of educational enrollment, as compared to its population, exceeded that of Nassau County, Roosevelt's lower educational achievement levels resulted in lower employment rates and higher representation in lower paying jobs. In 1990, the 661,486 Nassau County persons over 16 years of age in the workforce represented 51.4 percent of the population, as compared to

51.3 percent of Roosevelt's population of 7,711 persons. By 2000, a clear difference in workforce representation had emerged. Whereas the composition of the respective workforces had some similarities, those employed in the Nassau County economy had fallen to 47.3 percent of the population, as compared to 42.7 percent of Roosevelt residents. Of note is that despite decreasing from 1990, the reliance on government employment by Roosevelt residents exceeded those in Nassau County. Reasons for this include the relative stability of employment as well as a job that provides pension and health benefits.

Table 6: Workforce Employment - over 16 years of age

		1990		2000		Increase (Decrease)	
Nassau	Private wage and salary	511,645	77.3%	485,369	76.9%	(26,276)	(5.1%)
County:	Government	106,671	16.1%	108,083	17.1%	1,412	1.3%
	Self-employed	43,170	6.6%	37,736	6.0%	(5,434)	(12.6%)
	Total	661,486	100%	631,188	100%	(30,298)	(4.6%)
Roosevelt:	Private wage and salary	5,623	72.9%	5,245	77.4%	(378)	(6.7%)
	Government	1,822	23.6%	1,326	19.6%	(496)	(27.2%)
	Self-employed	266	3.5%	202	3.0%	(64)	(24.1%)
	Total	7,711	100%	6,773	100%	(938)	(12.2%)

Source: 1990 U.S Census Table DP-3, 2000 U.S. Census Table DP-3.

JOB SKILLS:

Employment of Nassau County and Roosevelt workers were comparable in most industry sectors, excepting for jobs in the professional, managerial and administrative categories. These jobs tend to require a higher degree of education, something achieved in greater percentages by the Nassau County workforce. Conversely, clerical, service and machine operators jobs, often requiring a lower degree of education, were the three largest categories employing Roosevelt residents.

Table 7: Employment by Industry Sector

	1990			
Industry Sector	Nassau County		Roosevelt	
Technician	20,753	3.1%	330	4.3%
Professional	115,951	17.5%	870	11.3%
Manager/Administrator	112,278	17.0%	667	8.6%
Sales	93,861	14.2%	525	6.8%
Clerical	130,222	19.7%	1,843	23.9%
Crafts/Construct/Mechanic	57,824	8.8%	586	7.6%
Machine Operators	17,761	2.7%	452	5.9%
Transportation Operators	19,174	2.9%	447	5.8%
Laborers	16,141	2.4%	262	3.4%
Farm	5,202	.8%	101	1.3%
Service	68,286	10.3%	1,524	19.8%
Private Household	4,033	.6%	104	1.3%
Total	661,486	100%	7,711	100%

Source: 1990 Census, Table DP-3, Labor Force Status and Employment Characteristics.

CHAPTER V

By 2000, the differing levels of educational attainment between Nassau County and Roosevelt residents had resulted in recognizable differences in labor force employment. The 2000 Nassau County labor force employment for those over 16 years old decreased by 4.6 percent to 631,188, and now represented 47.3 percent of the Nassau County population. Roosevelt's labor force was not so fortunate. The 6,773 persons in 2000 working represented 42.7 percent of Roosevelt's population, reflecting a disappointing 12.2 percent employment decrease from 1990. Additionally, those employed in private wage and salary jobs decreased by 6.7 percent, as compared to Nassau County's 5.1 percent drop. Government employment decreased by 27.2 percent; in contrast to the 1.3 percent growth in Nassau County. Entrepreneurs, the backbone of small business and critical to economic growth of any community, differed significantly between Nassau County and Roosevelt. In Nassau County, those self-employed decreased by 12.6 percent between 1990 and 2000, and now represented 6.0 percent of the workforce. As an example of two workforce sectors heading in different directions, Roosevelt self-employed individuals, already in short supply, decreased by 24.1 percent and represented only 3 percent of the workforce. Furthermore, the percent ratio between Nassau County and Roosevelt self-employed had increased from 1.89 to 1 in 1990 to 2 to 1 in 2000. In addition, the composition of the respective workforces also changed during the 10 years ending with 2000, and appears in the following analysis.

Table 7 (cont.): Employment by Industry Sector

	2000			
Industry Sector	**Nassau County**		**Roosevelt**	
Professional	74,934	11.9%	668	9.8%
Finance/Insur/Real Estate	72,942	11.6%	489	7.2%
Sales	94,803	15.0%	986	14.6%
Clerical/Information	25,825	4.1%	975	14.4%
Crafts/Construct/Mechanics	32,466	5.1%	284	4.2%
Machine Operators	40,795	6.5%	497	7.3%
Transportation Operators	38,099	6.0%	486	7.2%
Farm/Agric/Fish	635	.1 %	-0-	-0-%
Service	250,689	39.7%	2,388	35.3%
Total	631,188	100%	6,773	100%

Source: 2000 U.S. Census, Table DP-3.

Despite that the decrease between 1990 and 2000 of the Roosevelt workforce employment over 16 years of age was proportionately greater than Nassau County, the disparity in the distribution of jobs between the higher paying professional, managerial and administrative, crafts and construction sectors had narrowed. These jobs tend to require a higher degree of education and skills, areas in which Roosevelt had kept pace with Nassau County. Nassau County decreased professional jobs by 35.4 percent, managerial and administrative (now included in Fire, Insurance and Real Estate) by 35.0 percent and crafts and construction jobs by 43.9 percent. By comparison, Roosevelt lost 23.2 percent of its professional jobs, decreased managerial and administrative employment by 26.7 percent and lost 51.5 percent of its crafts and construction employment. In occupations where a lower level of education would be acceptable, such as clerical and service, Nassau County grew by 39.3 percent, while Roosevelt, in the aggregate, reported no growth at all. However, in sales jobs, Nassau County increased by one percent while Roosevelt reported 87.8 percent growth.

Furthermore, Roosevelt's labor force decreased at a greater percent than Nassau County's, with Roosevelt also reporting a higher degree of unemployment, when comparing those employed to those who are not.

Table 8: Employment Status - Male and Female - 16 years of age and older

		1990		2000		Increase (Decrease)	
Nassau	Males employed	364,292	55.1%	339,295	53.8%	(24,997)	(6.9%)
County:	Females employed	297,194	44.9%	291,893	46.2%	(5,301)	(1.8%)
	Total	661,486	100%	631,188	100%	(30,298)	(4.6%)
Roosevelt:	Males employed	3,735	48.4%	3,271	48.3%	(464)	(12.4%)
	Females employed	3,976	51.6%	3,502	51.7%	(474)	(11.9%)
	Total	7,711	100%	6,773	100%	(938)	(12.2%)

Source: 1990 U.S. Census Table DP-3, 2000 U.S. Census Tables DP-3.

In 1990, of the 661,486 persons over 16 years of age employed in Nassau County, 55.1 percent were male and 44.9 percent females, a 1.23 to 1 ratio. For the 7,711 persons over 16 employed in Roosevelt, 48.4 percent were male and 51.6 percent female, a .94 to 1 ratio. By 2000, males in the Nassau County workforce had decreased by 6.9 percent, falling to 53.8 percent of the employment base. Females, while decreasing by 1.8 percent, improved their labor force participation by 1.3 percent. The male to female ratio in the workforce had narrowed to 1.16 to 1. In contrast, Roosevelt lagged behind Nassau County with a disappointing 12.4 percent decrease in employed males and an 11.9 percent decrease in employed females. The result was that males and females employed in Roosevelt respectively remained at 48 and 51 percent of the labor force. As female headed families increased regionally, fewer females proportionally participated in the labor force decrease in Nassau County, as did in Roosevelt. An important distinction is that females represented a larger share of the decrease in the Roosevelt workforce while Nassau County females did not. Additionally, while there was a greater proportional labor force decrease in Roosevelt than in Nassau County, the male and female composition of the respective workforces, for the most part, remained unchanged.

As would also be expected, the relationship existing between the employment and unemployment status of males and females over 16 years of age was disproportionately favorable to Nassau County over Roosevelt.

Table 9: Unemployed Compared to Workforce (a)

		1990		2000		Increase (Decrease)	
Nassau County:	Total Workforce	690,066	100%	655,363	100%	(34,703)	(5.0%)
	Male unemployed	15,066	2.2%	12,807	2.0%	(2,259)	(15.0%)
	Female unemployed	13,514	2.0%	11,368	1.7%	(2,146)	(15.9%)
	Total	28,580	4.2%	24,175	3.7%	(4,405)	(15.4%)
Roosevelt:	Total Workforce	8,406	100%	7,237	100%	(1169)	(13.9%)
	Male unemployed	248	2.9%	273	3.8%	25	10.1%
	Female unemployed	447	5.3%	191	2.6%	(256)	(57.3%)
	Total	695	8.2%	464	6.4%	(231)	(33.2%)

Source: 1990 U.S. Census Table DP-3, 2000 U.S. Census Table DP-3.
Note (a): Workforce defined as employed plus unemployed.

The 1990 Nassau County unemployed represented 4.2 percent of the workforce, with males approximately 2.2 percent of their workforce force and females 2 percent. Roosevelt's 8.2 percent unemployment rate was nearly double that of Nassau County's, with males and females respectively representing 2.9 and 5.3 percent of Roosevelt's workforce. By 2000, the Nassau County unemployed decreased to 3.7 percent of the workforce, a 15.4 percent decline, while Roosevelt's unemployment rate fell by almost a third to 6.4 percent. The unemployment status of Nassau County males and females in 2000 each decreased to nearly 2 percent of their respective employment bases, with unemployed males and females decreasing respectively by 15 and 15.9 percent from 1990. In stark contrast, Roosevelt's male unemployed increased by 10.1 percent, while females decreased by 57.3 percent. Significant is that between 1990 and 2000 the Roosevelt unemployment fell slightly more than two times faster than Nassau County's rate. Also important was the fact that Roosevelt's workforce contracted nearly three times as fast as Nassau County's, and that the male unemployment rate by 2000 was nearly 2 times the Nassau County male unemployment rate.

A comparison between employed and unemployed reveals how Roosevelt had fared as compared to Nassau County. Between 1990 and 2000, the ratio of the 30,298 decrease in employment in the Nassau County economy for those 16 years of age and older, to the drop of 4,405 in unemployed was 6.88 to 1. While improving from 1990, Roosevelt's, net loss in employment of 938 resulted in a workforce where 4.06 persons were unemployed for every one not working. As a result, the ratio of employed to unemployed in Roosevelt, while improving between 1990 and 2000, still lagged behind Nassau County. In 1990, the Nassau County ratio was 23.2 persons employed to every person unemployed, with an 11.1 to 1 ratio in Roosevelt. By 2000, the Nassau County ratio improved to 26.1 to 1, while Roosevelt increased to 14.6 to 1. Roosevelt, while improving, remained a community of lower economic activity, surrounded by an economically vibrant Nassau County.

FAMILY INCOME:

The socioeconomic infrastructure of Roosevelt had weakened. Residents lagged behind Nassau County in academic attainment and job skills, resulting in a workforce that was forced to accept lower paying jobs. Furthermore, Roosevelt had nearly as many single parent households headed by females, as families headed by both husbands and wives.

With workers lacking the required skills for higher paying jobs, and having fewer wage earners in their families, a drawn conclusion is that Roosevelt family income would be less than that of Nassau County families. The following tables reflect how family income in Roosevelt, while improving between 1990 and 2000, still lagged behind family income growth for Nassau County.

Table 10: Nominal Family Income

Nominal Family Income	1990 Nassau County Families		Roosevelt Families	
$0-$5,000	4,247	1.2%	78	2.3%
$5,000-$9,999	4,733	1.4%	136	4.0%
$10,000-$14,999	7,557	2.2%	144	4.3%
$15,000-$24,999	24,082	6.9%	375	11.1%
$25,000-$49,999	89,077	25.7%	1,165	34.5%
$50,000 and over	217,094	62.6%	1,479	43.8%
Total	346,790	100%	3,377	100%

Nominal Family Income	2000 Nassau County Families		Roosevelt Families	
$0-$9,999	7,572	2.2%	153	4.5%
$10,000-$14,999	6,066	1.7%	160	4.7%
$15,000-$24,999	16,312	4.7%	276	8.0%
$25,000-$49,999	57,426	16.4%	863	25.1%
$50,000 and over	262,318	75.0%	1,979	57.7%
Total	349,694	100%	3,431	100%

Source: 1990 U.S. Census Table DP-4, Income and Poverty Status in 1989; 2000 U.S. Census Table DP-3, Profile of Selected Economic Characteristics: 2000.

In 1990, the 10.6 percent of Roosevelt families represented at the lower income categories exceeded the 4.8 percent of Nassau County families earning $15,000 or less. Fewer Roosevelt families also earned over $25,000, with 88.3 percent of Nassau County families earning in excess of $25,000, as compared to 78.3 percent for Roosevelt families. Furthermore, 43.8 percent of Roosevelt families earned over $50,000, while 62.6 percent of Nassau County families did. By 2000, correlating with the improving educational attainment, economic conditions slightly improved to where only 3.9 percent of Nassau County families and 9.2 percent of Roosevelt families were earning less than $15,000. Conditions also improved to where 91.4 percent of Nassau County families earned in excess of $25,000, followed by 82.8 percent of Roosevelt families. In part because more residents attended or graduated college, Nassau County families earning over $50,000 improved from 62.6 percent in 1990 to 75.0 percent in 2000. Furthermore, the gap between those earning over $100,000 annually had also narrowed. In 1990, the 19.6 percent rate of Nassau County families earning over $100,000 was triple the 6.3 percent of Roosevelt families. By 2000, Nassau County families earning over $100,000, while nearly doubling to 37.4 percent, were now just over twice the 17.6 percent of Roosevelt families earning over $100,000, a three-fold increase from 1990. Reflecting a lower percent of college attendees and graduates, Roosevelt families earning over $50,000 per year, while improving from 43.8 percent in 1990 to 57.7 percent by 2000, still lagged behind Nassau County.

Mean per capita and family median income distribution variances also existed between Nassau County and Roosevelt, and are presented in the following table.

Table 11: Mean Per Capita and Median Family (Nominal and Real) Income

		1990		2000	
		Mean Per Capita	Median Family	Mean Per Capita	Median Family
Nassau	Nominal $	$23,352	$60,619	$32,151	$81,246
County:	Real $ (1)	$16,873	$43,800	$17,588	$44,445
Roosevelt:	Nominal $	$12,955	$45,297	$16,950	$56,380
	Real $ (1)	$9,361	$32,729	$9,272	$30,842

Source: 1990 U.S. Census Table DP-4, 2000 U.S. Census Table DP-3.
Note (1): Based on 1984 CPI as the base year, New York Area Index as of July 1990 and July 2000.

The 1990 Roosevelt mean per capita and median family incomes, expressed in both nominal and real dollars, were respectively 55 and 75 percent of their Nassau County equivalent. This gap became progressively worse by 2000. The Nassau County nominal mean per capita and median family incomes experienced a respective 38 and 34 percent growth between 1990 and 2000, while mean per capita and median incomes expressed in real dollars grew by 4.2 and 1.4 percent respectively. The growth of Roosevelt's mean per capita and median family incomes expressed in nominal dollars lagged behind at 31 and 25 percent, with mean per capita and median income expressed in real dollars not only lagging behind, but actually decreasing by 1 and 6 percent respectively. The Roosevelt mean per capita and median family incomes expressed in both nominal and real dollars had now having fallen to 53 and 69 percent of their Nassau County equivalents. Not only had Roosevelt failed to keep up with Nassau County, but it actually lost economic ground.

HOUSING:

As would be expected, with the additional costs of home ownership, including down payment requirements, the lower mean per capita and median family incomes in Roosevelt impacted the incidence of home ownership.

Table 12: Occupied Housing Units

		1990		2000		Increase (Decrease)	
Nassau	Total occupied units	431,515	100%	447,387	100%	15,872	3.7%
County:	Owner occupied	347,143	80.4%	359,264	80.3%	12,121	3.5%
	Renter occupied	84,372	19.6%	88,123	19.7%	3,751	4.4%
Roosevelt:	Total occupied units	3,849	100%	4,061	100%	212	5.5%
	Owner occupied	2,907	75.5%	2,998	73.8%	91	3.1%
	Renter occupied	942	24.5%	1,063	26.2%	121	12.8%

Source: 1990 U.S. Census Table DP-1, 2000 U.S. Census Tables DP-1.

In 1990, of the total occupied housing units in Nassau County, 80.4 percent were owner occupied and 19.6 percent renter occupied. Of Roosevelt's total occupied housing units, 75.5 percent were owner occupied with 24.5 percent renter occupied. By 2000, total Nassau County housing units had increased by 3.7 percent, with 76 percent of the increase owner occupied units, and 24 percent renter occupied. In Roosevelt, the total occupied housing units increased by 5.5 percent, with 43 percent of the increase owner occupied units, and 57 percent renter occupied. While Nassau County experienced a respective 3.5 and 4.4 percent balanced increase in owner and renter occupied housing units, what occurred in Roosevelt was a disparity in growth between owner and renter occupied housing units, which increased by 3.1 and 12.8 percent respectively. Nassau County's growth in owner occupied housing units had lagged slightly behind that of renter occupied units, while the opposite was occurring in Roosevelt where renter occupied housing units grew at a rate four times faster than owner occupied units.

In a trend that continued between 1990 and 2000, the 1990 median gross rent in Roosevelt of $661, was slightly less than the Nassau County median gross rent of $678. By 2000, the median gross rent of Roosevelt had increased 45 percent to $960, as compared to the 42 percent increase in Nassau County's median gross rent to $964 (1990 U.S. Census, table DP-1, 2000 U.S. Census table DP-4). Interestingly, despite lower incomes, renters in Roosevelt continued to pay almost as much rent as Nassau County as a whole.

SUMMARY:

Of all the socioeconomic indicators discussed above, family structure and academic attainment, workforce participation, jobs skills, household income, and home ownership, Roosevelt started from a less favorable position compared to Nassau County as a whole. During the 10-year period covered by this research, in comparison to the surrounding Nassau County, Roosevelt has:

(1) become a more concentrated and racially segregated black community, despite experiencing population growth at approximately the same rate as Nassau County;

(2) experienced a decrease in families with a male and female present, and had more families headed by women than men;

(3) had a breakdown of traditional family structure, where there are more single males and females as married males and females;

(4) had slower growth in college enrollments, with greater student enrollment in elementary and high school;

(5) slower growth in post-secondary education attainment;

(6) had a decrease in self-employed entrepreneurs, an increase in private sector employment, and a decrease government employment;

(7) had a decrease, or negligible growth in higher paying professional, craft, construction, and machine operator jobs, and an increase in lower paying service, clerical, and sales jobs;

(8) experienced a much sharper growth in both male and female unemployment;

(9) had growth in nominal median family and mean per capita income, yet a

majority of families were still earning nominal income below $56,380 as compared to approximately $81,246 for Nassau County;

(10)   had mean per capita and median real family income grow at a slower rate than Nassau County's, with decrease in Roosevelt's real mean per capita income;

(11)   had a modest increase in owner occupied housing units and a sharper increase in renter occupied units; the opposite being true for Nassau County.

Overall, despite experiencing some growth between 1990 and 2000, Roosevelt had not kept pace with surrounding Nassau County. What is also clear is that the Roosevelt workforce was dealt a set back by the changing skills required of the global economy.

The results of this study uncovers very similar results as Huntington Station and North Amityville experienced, and similarly the remaining sections of this study present suggested Roosevelt business district and community revitalization strategies that can tap into Roosevelt's economic development potential.

ROOSEVELT'S BUSINESS DISTRICT: TAPPING AN ECONOMIC RESOURCE

As Andreaus 13 noted, economic development depends on people. Overcoming the existing institutional racism structure will depend strongly on the strategic partnerships that the Roosevelt community can make with the white community and will rely heavily on the talent and perseverance of the community. That will make any economic development successes lasting, and not rely upon the economic development provided by structures and buildings that ultimately erode over time. The presented socioeconomic profile of Roosevelt, while weaker than Nassau County, provides opportunities for economic growth. With this in mind, improvements for the Roosevelt business district should take advantage of the competitive advantages of the community. The strategy should address a variety of needs, such as:

(a)   **An entrepreneurial class** that decreased by 24.1 percent from 1990, to where Roosevelt entrepreneurs, as part of the Roosevelt workforce, are now 50% of the ratio that Nassau County's entrepreneurs are to the Nassau County workforce. This would indicate that there is growth potential in Roosevelt's entrepreneurial class, in as every community has untapped entrepreneurs, each representing a potential business.

(b)   **A local workforce with potential to improve earnings.** Roosevelt's workforce is burdened with a family structure where more single males and females head households with children under 18 than married males and females. Furthermore, the single-family heads are a greater percentage of total Roosevelt families than their Nassau County counterparts. Roosevelt's weakened family structure is the result of a decade where families with both a male and female present decreased, resulting in more families headed by women than men. Why this matters is that single-family heads not only have income earning responsibilities, but also have child care concerns as well. Providing daycare support would allow single family heads to either seek higher paying jobs, or become employed, thereby reducing Roosevelt's proportionately higher unemployment rate of males and females.

(c) **Housing** in Roosevelt, while in greater supply for homeowners than renters, still reflects the need for home ownership, given the sharper increase in renter occupied units than owner occupied. That improvement is achievable is evident, when compared to Nassau County where owner occupied units' represent a greater share of occupied housing units than rental units. Building housing units on Nassau Road can transform Roosevelt into a 24-hour community, a necessary element in any revitalization process. The attracting of young people to live on Nassau Road will bring more pedestrian traffic, and potential consumers, to the Roosevelt business district.

(d) **Median Family income** and mean per capita income in Roosevelt is below that of Nassau County, further compounding a decade long slide in Roosevelt's mean per capita income. One cause is the slow adaptation of Roosevelt's workforce to Long Island's changing job market, caused in part by the globalization of the world's economy and the impact of that change on the Long Island economy. Contributing to the lower median family income are the combination of more female family heads who traditionally earn lower salaries than their male counterparts, and the Roosevelt workforce's lower educational attainment levels, often making access to the higher paying jobs in the global marketplace more difficult. This situation can be improved with a coordinated policy that addresses aspects of job training and workforce support.

What as been uncovered in the communities of color that have been discussed, (North Amityville, Huntington Station and Roosevelt) as compared to each respective surrounding county, is a pattern of weaknesses in education attainment, job creation, entrepreneurism, job skills required of the global economy, accessing the higher paying jobs in the Long Island economy, household structure, household income, and housing needs. Would a predominantly white community in Nassau County fare better or worse? The following analysis of greater Port Washington will shed light on that.

CHAPTER V

Chapter VI

PORT WASHINGTON:
A COMMUNITY WEATHERING GLOBALIZATION

There seems to have been little residual negative economic impact experienced by Port Washington's highly educated workforce from the deindustrialization of Long Island's manufacturing base, or from the contraction of the region's defense industry. This was unlike the workforce reductions at Long Island's many machine shops that impacted much of the regions less skilled and less educated workers. At the same time, benefiting Port Washington was the growing demand for more skilled and more educated workers in Long Island's emerging high technology and expanding financial and banking sectors. The result was that globalization of economic activity between 1970 and 1990 impacted the Port Washington peninsula (Zip Code 11050) unlike North Amityville, Huntington Station, and Roosevelt. Additionally, Port Washington fared better between 1990 and 2000 as compared to the surrounding Nassau County.

The analysis of this period of industrial and economic restructuring comparing Port Washington with surrounding Nassau County includes: the Port Washington workforce and related economy; the cost to the community of the loss of jobs requiring a lower level of education, such as blue-collar manufacturing and clerical; the Port Washington residents ability to achieve the education and skills necessary for employment in the region's emerging higher paying technology jobs, specialized financial services, and computer and telecommunication technology and their related commercial applications; the global economy and changes in technology, now requiring more intellectual skills; and the correlation between education and family income as compared to past years.

All these questions will be explored by comparing the socio-economic effects of globalization and technological change on and between Nassau County and Port Washington.

PORT WASHINGTON: A WORKFORCE FOR THE GLOBAL ECONOMY

The socio economic evolution of Port Washington was quite different from what has characterized Nassau County during the 10 years spanning 1990 and 2000.

There has been an increase in married households, with single headed households decreasing to where they represent nearly 1 in 7 families, 29 percent less than the 1 in 5 family rate of Nassau County. While the educational enrollment in advanced grades are slightly below Nassau County, overall educational attainment levels are greater in Port Washington, and in part explain the modestly larger increase in Port Washington employment levels as compared to Nassau County. The Port Washington unemployment rates were lower, and labor participation rates were higher, than surrounding Nassau County, with the Port Washington workforce more widely employed in professional jobs requiring greater skills than in Nassau County.

Surprisingly, significantly fewer Port Washington residents owned their own homes than in surrounding Nassau County, while those living in rental apartments and paying comparably higher rents were 70 percent more than the percent of those living in renter occupied units in Nassau County. The following comparison of a broad range of social indicators and economic data shows how Port Washington, a relatively affluent Long Island north shore community, fared as compared to Nassau County.

POPULATION
Table 1: Racial Composition

		1990		2000		Increase (Decrease)	
Nassau	Total	1,287,348	100%	1,334,544	100%	47,196	3.7%
County:	White	1,115,119	86.6%	1,058,285	79.3%	(56,834)	(5.1%)
(a)	Black	111,057	8.6%	134,673	10.1%	23,616	21.3%
	Other (a)	61,172	4.8%	141,586	10.6%	80,414	131.5%
Port	Total	28,241	100%	28,551	100%	310	1.1%
Washington:	White	24,756	87.7%	23,938	83.8%	(818)	(3.3%)
(b)	Black	620	2.2%	589	2.1%	(31)	(5.0%)
	Other	2,865	10.1%	4,024	14.1%	1,159	40.5%

Source: (a) 1990 U.S. Census, Table DP-1., 2000 U. S. Census, Table DP-1.
      (b) Infoshare.org. 1990 U.S. Census Table: Population by Race; 2000 U.S. Census Table: Race.

Note (1): Other includes Natural Americans, Asians and Pacific Islander, and in 2000 other race persons/two or more race persons.

The total Nassau County population grew by 3.7 percent between 1990 and 2000, to a total of 1,334,544, whereas by 2000, the Port Washington community reported growth of 1.1 percent to 28,551. While the population growth percentages were similar, the changes in their racial composition were not. In 1990, whites and blacks respectively represented 86.6 and 8.6 percent of Nassau County's population. By 2000 the black component of Nassau County's population had increased to 10.1 percent, while whites decreased to 79.3 percent; the non-white non-black population (termed other) rose from 4.8 percent to 10.6 percent. Blacks grew at a faster pace; increasing by 21.3 percent or 23,616 persons to 134,673, while Whites decreasing by 56,834 people, fell by 5.1 percent.

Between 1990 and 2000, while the total population of Port Washington marginally increased, black residents did not. In 1990, the Port Washington population was 87.7 percent white and 2.2 percent black. By 2000, the Port Washington population of 28,551 represented growth of 1.1 percent, with "other" accounting for all the growth. The white population had decreased by 3.3 percent, with those remaining representing 83.8 percent of the Port Washington population. Others, including Asian and Pacific Islanders and persons of two or more races increased by 40.5 percent to 4,024 persons, and now represented 14.1 percent of the population. Blacks, while decreasing 5.0 percent to 589, were 2.1 percent of Port Washington's population, leaving the black community of Port Washington virtually unchanged from 1990. In contrast, while Nassau County as a whole appeared slightly more integrated, Long Island communities where black majorities exist, as shown previously, actually became more segregated.

FAMILY STRUCTURE:
Table 2: Family Composition (with children under 18 years of age)

		1990		2000		Increase (Decrease)	
Nassau	Total Families	344,502	100%	347,026	100%	2,524	.7%
County:	Husband/Wife	286,638	83.2%	282,126	81.3%	(4,512)	(1.6%)
(a)	Male head	13,914	4.0%	15,958	4.6%	2,044	14.7%
	Female head	43,950	12.8%	48,942	14.1%	4,992	11.4%
	Persons per family	2.94		3.34		.4	13.6%
Port	Total Families	7,758	100%	7,799	100%	41	.5%
Washington:	Husband/Wife	6,378	82.2%	6,647	85.2%	269	4.2%
(b)	Male head	351	4.5%	270	3.5%	(81)	(23.1%)
	Female head	1,029	13.3%	882	11.3%	(147)	(14.3%)
	Persons per family	3.64		3.66		.02	.5%

Source: (a) 1990 U.S. Census Table DP-1, 2000 Census Table DP-1.
      (b) Infoshare.org. 1990 and 2000 U.S. Census Table: Family Type and Children under 18.

Changes in family composition between 1990 and 2000 reflected greater structural weakening of the two-parent household in Nassau County than in Port Washington. As shown in Table 2, single parent families, as a percent of all single parent families, decreased a combined 16.5 percent in Port Washington, as compared to the 12.2 percent growth rate in Nassau County. However, as an example of two communities heading in somewhat different directions, between 1990 and 2000 two-parent families with children under 18 increased by 4.2 percent in Port Washington and decreased by 1.6 percent in Nassau County as a whole. By 2000, 18.7 percent of families with children in the greater Nassau County had single parent households, compared to 16.8 percent one decade earlier. In Port Washington, 1990 single-family households were 17.8 percent of all households, falling 16.9 percent to 14.8 percent by 2000.

Reflecting a somewhat weaker family structure in Nassau County, in 2000 85.9 percent of families with children under than 18 years of age had a male present, while a male presence was reported in 88.7 percent of Port Washington families. For Nassau County this represented a decrease from 1990, where 87.2 percent of its families had a male present, while Port Washington demonstrated an increase from 1990 where 86.7 percent of its families had a male presence. The average 1990 Port Washington family size of 3.64 persons was 23.8 percent more crowded than the 2.94 persons in the average Nassau County family. By 2000, family demographics had changed. Families in Port Washington with a husband and wife had increased by 4.2 percent, male headed families decreased by 23.1 percent, and families headed by females decreased by 14.3 percent. Similar to families with children under 18 in Nassau County, which experienced a .7 percent growth between 1990 and 2000, families in Port Washington increased by a meager .5 percent to 7,799. While there was little growth in total Nassau County families, the average 2000 family became larger, increasing by 13.6 percent from 1990 to 3.34 persons per family. In contrast, family size in Port Washington grew by .5 percent to 3.66 by 2000.

Table 3: Marital Status (those 15 years of age and older)

		1990		2000		Increase (Decrease)	
Nassau	Total Males	501,794	100 %	469,049	100%	(32,745)	(6.5%)
County:	Single Males	202,633	40.4%	173,390	37.0%	(29,243)	(14.4%)
(a)	Married Males	299,161	59.6%	295,659	63.0%	(3,502)	(1.2%)
	Total Females	553,856	100%	589,567	100%	35,711	6.4%
	Single Females	255,156	46.1%	257,499	43.7%	2,343	.9%
	Married Females	298,700	53.9%	332,068	56.3%	33,368	11.2%
Port	Total Males	11,226	100%	10,710	100%	(516)	(4.6%)
Washington:	Single Males	4,395	39.2%	3,633	33.9%	(762)	(17.3%)
(b)	Married Males	6,831	60.8%	7,077	66.1%	246	3.6%
	Total Females	12,216	100%	11,796	100%	(420)	(3.4%)
	Single Females	5,333	43.7%	4,608	39.1%	(725)	(13.6%)
	Married Females	6,883	56.3%	7,188	60.9%	305	4.4%

Source: (a)1990 U.S.Census of Population-NYS Data Center, 2000 U.S. Census Table DP-2.
(b) Infoshare.org. 1990 U.S. Census Table: Population by Marital Status; 2000 U. S. Census Table: Marital Status by Sex.

Integral to family structure stability is the marital status of men and women. In 1990, 59.6 percent of the males living in Nassau County older than 15 years of age were married while 40.4 percent were single. Similarly, 46.1 percent of women were single with 53.9 percent married. By 2000, males had decreased by 6.5 percent, with single males dropping by 14.4 percent and married males falling at a slower 1.2 percent rate. Single males over 15 now represented 37 percent of males, with married males increasing to 63 percent. In similar fashion, by 2000, single females over 15 living in Nassau County had marginally increased by .9 percent, and now represented 43.7 percent of females. In contrast, married females growing by a much faster 11.2 percent rate, increased to 56.3 percent of Nassau County females.

Between 1990 and 2000, except for total females, single and married males and females over 15 years of age living in Port Washington followed a pattern comparable to Nassau County. While Nassau County males decreased by 6.5 percent and females grew by 6.4 percent, Port Washington males fell by 4.6 percent, with females decreasing by 3.4 percent. There were however differences in the composition of that decrease. That Nassau County single males decreased by 14.4 percent from 1990, and single females remained basically unchanged, could explain the 11.2 percent increase in married females over 15. Similarly, Port Washington married males and females increased by 3.6 and 4.4 percent respectively, while both single males and females respectively decreased by 17.3 and 13.6 percent. There was also evidence of the improvement and strengthening of the Port Washington family structure, with a 4.2 percent growth in families with both a male and female present, while Nassau County reported a 1.6 percent decline. In 1990, 39.2 percent of Port Washington males were single, with 60.8 percent married, while 43.7 percent of females were single and 56.3 percent married. By 2000, reflecting the increase in Port Washington married males and females, of the males, 33.9 percent were single and 66.1 percent were married, while 39.1 percent of females were single and 60.9 percent were married. By 2000 in Nassau County, 63 percent of males and 56.3 percent of females were married, increasing from 1990 levels of 59.6 and 53.9 percent respectively.

ACADEMIC ACHIEVEMENT:

As previously shown a correlation exists between academic achievement and higher family income, and that those advancing to higher education have an opportunity to work in higher paying jobs. Such a correlation developed between 1990 and 2000, where both similarities and differences in the pattern of school enrollment and in educational achievement between Nassau County and Port Washington emerged and appears in Table 4.

Table 4: School Enrollment (3 years of age and older)

		1990		2000		Increase (Decrease)	
Nassau	Preliminary	27,741	8.8%	30,116	8.4%	2,375	8.6%
County:	Elementary-H.S.	187,696	59.0%	246,184	68.8%	58,488	31.2%
(a)	College	102,438	32.2%	81,375	22.8%	(21,063)	(20.6%)
	Total	317,875	100%	357,675	100%	39,800	12.5%
Port	Preliminary	582	8.6%	772	10.7%	190	32.7%
Washington:	Elementary-H.S	4,099	60.6%	5,084	70.4%	985	24.0%
(b)	College	2,079	30.8%	1,363	18.9%	(716)	(34.4%)
	Total	6,760	100%	7,219	100%	459	6.8%

Source: (a) 1990 U.S. Census Table DP-2; 2000 U.S. Census Table DP-2.
   (b) Infoshare.org. 1990 U.S. Census Table: School enrollment and Type; 2000 U.S. Census Table: School Enrollment, Level and Type of school by Sex.

In 1990, while Nassau County and Port Washington exhibited similar patterns of school enrollment, there were discernible differences in the distribution of that enrollment. Of the 317,875 persons over 3 years of age enrolled in Nassau County schools, 8.8 percent were enrolled in preliminary schools, 59 percent were in elementary through high school, and 32.2 percent were attending college. By comparison, of the 6,760 Port Washington school enrollees, 8.6 percent attended preliminary schools, 60.6 percent were enrolled in elementary through high school, and 30.8 percent were attending college. By 2000, the differing patterns widened slightly between those enrolled in elementary through high school and those attending college. In Nassau County, of the 357,675 persons attending school, 8.4 percent were in preliminary schools, 68.8 percent were in elementary through high school, and 22.8 percent were attending college. Of the 7,219 students in Port Washington, 10.7 percent were in preliminary schools, 70.4 percent were enrolled in elementary through high school, and 18.9 percent were attending college. There was however an enrollment gap developing by 2000, where 77.2 percent of Nassau County school enrollees were in preliminary through high school, as compared to 81.1 percent in Port Washington, while the 22.8 percent of those in Nassau County attending college exceeded the 18.9 percent in Port Washington. The higher educational enrollment gap was explained in part by the fact that those in Port Washington attending college decreased by 34.4 percent between 1990 and 2000, a larger percentage decline than the 20.6 percent drop in Nassau County. The importance of college enrollment for both Nassau County and Port Washington residents is that as Table 1 in Chapter II indicates, a correlation exists between higher levels of education attained and increased household income. That Port Washington's growth in preliminary through high school enrollment exceeded Nassau

County, with college enrollment keeping pace with Nassau County, while still lagging behind, would indicate that increased future household incomes could be anticipated in Port Washington, providing that students return to their community.

Table 5: Educational Attainment - over 25 years of age

		1990		2000		Increase (Decrease)	
Nassau	8th Grade or less	52,599	6.0%	47,776	5.2%	(4,823)	(9.2%)
County:	9-12 gr. no diploma	86,546	9.8%	72,962	8.0%	(13,584)	(15.7%)
(a)	High School Grad	266,264	30.2%	243,454	26.8%	(22,810)	(8.6%)
	College 1-3 yrs.	211,557	24.0%	223,180	24.6%	11,623	5.5%
	College Grad +	264,071	30.0%	321,321	35.4%	57,250	21.7%
	Total	881,037	100%	908,693	100%	27,656	3.1%
Port	8th Grade or less	1,145	5.8%	974	4.8%	(171)	(14.9%)
Washington:	9-12 gr. no diploma	1,387	7.0%	947	4.7%	(440)	(31.7%)
(b)	High School Grad.	4,366	21.9%	3,753	18.6%	(613)	(14.0%)
	College 1-3 yrs.	3,216	16.2%	3,761	18.7%	545	16.9%
	College Grad +	9,780	49.1%	10,727	53.2%	947	9.7%
	Total	19,894	100%	20,162	100%	268	1.35%

Source: (a) 1990 U.S. Census Table DP-2, 2000 U.S. Census Table DP-2.
      (b) Infoshare.org. 1990 U. S. Census Table: Educational Attainment25+ yrs; 2000 U.S. Census
      Table: Educational Attainment for Persons 25+ Yrs by Sex.

By 1990, a 3 percent educational attainment gap had developed between Port Washington and Nassau County. While 68.4 and 70.4 percent of the respective 1990 Nassau County and Port Washington populations had completed some level of schooling, 84.2 percent of those over 25 years of age in Nassau County had graduated high school or gone on to higher education as compared to 87.2 percent in Port Washington. By 2000, those over 25 years of age having attained some level of education remained basically unchanged at 68.1 and 70.6 percent of the respective Nassau County and Port Washington populations. By 2000, Port Washington's higher education attainment gap had grown to 3.7 percent, with 86.8 percent of those in Nassau County graduating high school and going on to higher education, as compared to 90.5 percent in Port Washington. More revealing is the increase in the Port Washington higher educational attainment gap. By 2000 those in Port Washington attaining college were 71.9 percent of total educational attainment, increasing from 65.3 percent in 1990. In contrast, those in Nassau County over 25 years of age attaining college increased from 54.0 percent in 1990 to 60 percent by 2000. The gap between Port Washington and Nassau County had grown by 5 percent from 11.3 percent in 1990 to 11.9 percent by 2000.

The importance of the widening higher education attainment gap is that it occurred after changes in the global economy restructured the job market from jobs requiring a lesser degree of education and skills to jobs requiring a higher level. While there was comparable growth in college and post college educational attainment between Port Washington and Nassau County, the 50.7 percent of Port Washington residents attaining higher education levels by 2000 exceeded the 40.8 percent of the Nassau County population, drawing the correlation that a greater proportion of the Port Washington population was employed in higher paying jobs, resulting in greater family income, as is confirmed in Tables 10 and 11.

WORKFORCE EMPLOYMENT:

A correlation was found to exist between the higher levels of educational attainment achieved by Port Washington residents, their higher workforce employment rates, and their greater representation in higher paying jobs. While Port Washington's percent distribution of educational enrollment was comparable to that of Nassau County, Port Washington's higher educational achievement levels have resulted in higher employment rates and greater representation in higher paying jobs. In 1990, the 661,486 Nassau County persons over 16 years of age in the workforce represented 51.4 percent of the population, as compared to Port Washington's 15,502 person workforce representing 54.9 percent of its population of 28,241 persons. By 2000, while the composition of the respective workforces had some similarities, employed Nassau County and Port Washington residents had fallen to 47.3 and 49.5 percent of their respective populations. Of note is that despite increasing slightly from 1990, the reliance on government employment by Nassau County residents exceeded those in Port Washington. As previously discussed, reasons for this include the relative stability of employment as well as jobs that provide pension and health benefits.

Table 6: Workforce Employment - over 16 years of age

		1990		2000		Increase (Decrease)	
Nassau	Private wage & salary	511,645	77.3%	485,369	76.9%	(26,276)	(5.1%)
County:	Government	106,671	16.1%	108,083	17.1%	1,412	1.3%
(a)	Self-employed	43,170	6.6%	37,736	6.0%	(5,434)	(12.6%)
	Total	661,486	100%	631,188	100%	(30,298)	(4.6%)
Port	Private wage & salary	12,084	78.0%	9,760	69.0%	(2,324)	(19.2%)
Washington:	Government	1,705	11.0%	1,861	13.2%	156	9.2%
(b)	Self-employed	1,713	11.0%	2,522	17.8%	809	47.2%
	Total	15,502	100%	14,143	100%	(1,359)	(8.8%)

Source: (a) 1990 U.S Census Table DP-3, 2000 U.S. Census Table DP-3.
      (b) Infoshare.org, 1990 U.S. Census Table: Type of Employer of Worker; 2000 U.S. Census Table: Industry by Type of Worker by Sex.

JOB SKILLS:

Employment of Nassau County and Port Washington workers were comparable in most industry sectors, excepting for jobs in the professional, managerial and administrative categories. These jobs tend to require a higher degree of education, something achieved in greater percentages by the Port Washington workforce. Conversely, after professional and managerial/administration, clerical, service and sales jobs, often requiring a lower degree of education, were the three largest categories employing Nassau County residents.

Table 7: Employment by Occupation Sector – Over 16 Years of Age

Occupation Sector	1990			
	Nassau County (a)		Port Washington (b)	
Technician	20,753	3.1%	356	2.3%
Professional	115,951	17.5%	3,290	21.2%
Manager/Administrator	112,278	17.0%	3,301	21.3%
Sales	93,861	14.2%	2,469	15.9%
Clerical	130,222	19.7%	2,243	14.5%
Crafts/Construct/Mechanic	57,824	8.8%	1,186	7.7%
Machine Operators	17,761	2.7%	376	2.4%
Transportation Operators	19,174	2.9%	268	1.7%
Laborers	16,141	2.4%	299	1.9%
Farm	5,202	.8%	185	1.2%
Service	68,286	10.3%	1,270	8.2%
Private Household	4,033	.6%	259	1.7%
Total	661,486	100%	15,502	100%

Source: (a) 1990 Census, Table DP-3, Labor Force Status and Employment Characteristics.
(b) Infoshare.org. 1990 U.S. Census Table: Occupation; 2000 U.S. Census Table: Occupation by Sex.

By 2000, the differing levels of educational attainment between Nassau County and Port Washington residents had resulted in recognizable differences in labor force employment. The 2000 Nassau County labor force employment for those over 16 years old decreased by 4.6 percent to 631,188, and now represented 47.3 percent of the Nassau County population. Port Washington's labor force of 14,143 persons in 2000 represented 49.5 percent of Port Washington's population, reflecting an 8.8 percent employment decrease from 1990, nearly twice the Nassau County decline. Additionally, those in Port Washington employed in private wage and salary jobs decreased by 19.2 percent, as compared to Nassau County's 5.1 percent decline. Government employment increased by 9.2 percent; as compared to the 1.3 percent growth in Nassau County. Entrepreneurs, the backbone of small business and critical to economic growth of any community, differed significantly between Nassau County and Port Washington. In Nassau County, those self-employed decreased by 12.6 percent between 1990 and 2000, and now represented 6.0 percent of the workforce. As an example of two workforce employment sectors heading in different directions, Port Washington's self-employed individuals, reflecting adaptability to the global economy, increased by 47.2 percent and now represented 17.8 percent of the workforce, increasing from 11 percent in 1990. Furthermore, the percent ratio between Port Washington and Nassau County self-employed had increased from 1.67 to 1 in 1990 to 2.97 to 1 by 2000. In addition, the composition of the respective workforces also changed during the 10 years ending with 2000, and appears in the following analysis.

Table 7 (cont.) Employment by Occupation Sector – Over 16 Years of Age

Occupation Sector	2000 Nassau County (a)		Port Washington (b)	
Professional	74,934	11.9%	3,350	23.7%
Finance/Insur/Real Estate	72,942	11.6%	646	4.5%
Sales	94,803	15.0%	2,079	14.7%
Clerical/Information	25,825	4.1%	1,523	10.8%
Crafts/Construct/Mechanics	32,466	5.1%	536	3.8%
Machine Operators	40,795	6.5%	355	2.5%
Transportation Operators	38,099	6.0%	376	2.7%
Farm/Agric/Fish	635	.1%	15	.1%
Service	250,689	39.7%	5,263	37.2%
Total	631,188	100%	14,143	100%

Source: (a) 2000 U.S. Census, Table DP-3.
(b) Infoshare.org, 1990 U.S. Census Table: Occupation; 2000 U.S. Census Table: Occupation by Sex.

Despite that the decrease between 1990 and 2000 of Port Washington's workforce employment over 16 years of age was greater than Nassau County, the disparity in the distribution of jobs between the higher paying professional, managerial and administrative, crafts and construction sectors had narrowed. These jobs tend to require a higher degree of education and skills, areas in which Port Washington exceeded Nassau County. Nassau County decreased professional jobs by 35.4 percent, managerial and administrative (now included in Fire, Insurance and Real Estate) by 35.0 percent and crafts and construction jobs by 43.9 percent. By comparison, Port Washington lost 39.4 percent of its professional, managerial and administrative jobs, and lost 54.8 percent of its crafts and construction employment. In occupations where a lower level of education is acceptable, such as clerical and service, Nassau County grew by 39.3 percent, while Port Washington grew by 93 percent. However, in sales jobs, Nassau County increased by one percent while Port Washington reported 15.8 percent decline.

Furthermore, Port Washington's labor force decreased at a greater percent than Nassau County's, with Nassau County reporting a slightly higher degree of unemployment, when comparing those employed to those who are not.

Table 8: Employment Status - Male and Female - 16 years of age and older

		1990		2000		Increase (Decrease)	
Nassau	Males employed	364,292	55.1%	339,295	53.8%	(24,997)	(6.9%)
County:	Females employed	297,194	44.9%	291,893	46.2%	(5,301)	(1.8%)
(a)	Total	661,486	100%	631,188	100%	(30,298)	(4.6%)
Port	Males employed	8,639	55.7%	7,781	55%	(858)	(9.9%)
Washington:	Females employed	6,863	44.3%	6,362	45%	(501)	(7.3%)
(b)	Total	15,502	100%	14,143	100%	(1,359)	(8.8%)

Source: (a) 1990 U.S. Census Table DP-3, 2000 U.S. Census Tables DP-3.
(b) Infoshare.org. 1990 U.S. Census Table: Sex and Employment Status; 2000 U.S. Census Table: Employment Status in 1999 by Sex.

CHAPTER VI

In 1990, of the 661,486 persons over 16 years of age employed in Nassau County, 55.1 percent were male and 44.9 percent females, a 1.23 to1 ratio. For the 15,502 persons over 16 employed in Port Washington, 55.7 percent were male and 44.3 percent female, a 1.26 to 1 ratio. By 2000, males in the Nassau County workforce had decreased by 6.9 percent, falling to 53.8 percent of the employment base. Females, while decreasing by 1.8 percent, improved their labor force participation by 1.3 percent. The male to female ratio in the workforce had narrowed to 1.16 to 1. In contrast, Port Washington lagged behind Nassau County with a 9.9 percent decrease in employed males and a 7.3 percent decrease in employed females. The result was that males and females employed in Port Washington respectively remained at 55 and 45 percent of the labor force, with the employment ratio of males to females narrowing to 1.22 to 1. As female headed families increased region- ally, fewer females proportionally participated in the labor force decrease in Nassau County, as did in Port Washington. However, employed females in the Port Washington workforce were comparable to Nassau County employed females. Additionally, while there was a greater proportional workforce decrease in Port Washington than in Nassau County, the male and female composition of the respective workforces, for the most part, remained comparable and unchanged.

As would also be expected, the relationship existing between the employment and unemployment status of males and females over 16 years of age was relatively compara- ble between Nassau County and Port Washington.

Table 9: Unemployed Compared to Workforce (c)

		1990		2000		Increase (Decrease)	
Nassau	Total Workforce	690,066	100%	655,363	100%	(34,703)	(5.0%)
County:	Male unemployed	15,066	2.2%	12,807	2.0%	(2,259)	(15.0%)
(a)	Female unemployed	13,514	2.0%	11,368	1.7%	(2,146)	(15.9%)
	Total	28,580	4.2%	24,175	3.7%	(4,405)	(15.4%)
Port	Total Workforce	16,108	100%	14,580	100%	(1,528)	(9.5%)
Washington:	Male unemployed	360	2.2%	235	1.6%	(125)	(34.7%)
(b)	Female unemployed	246	1.5%	202	1.4%	(44)	(17.9%)
	Total	606	3.7%	437	3.0%	(169)	(27.9%)

Source: (a) 1990 U.S. Census Table DP-3, 2000 U.S. Census Table DP-3.
     (b) Infoshare.org. 1990 U.S. Census Table: Sex and Employment Status; 2000 U.S. Census Table: Employment Status in 1999 by Sex.
Note (c): Workforce defined as employed plus unemployed.

The 1990 Nassau County unemployed represented 4.2 percent of the workforce, with males 2.2 percent and females 2 percent. Port Washington's 3.7 percent unemployment rate was below that of Nassau County's, with males and females respectively representing 2.2 and 1.5 percent of Port Washington's workforce. By 2000, the Nassau County unem- ployment rate decreased to 3.7 percent of the workforce, a 15.4 percent decline, while Port Washington's unemployment rate fell by 27.9 percent to 3.0 percent. The unemployment status of Nassau County males and females in 2000 each decreased to nearly 2 percent of their respective employment bases, with unemployed males and females decreasing respectively by 15 and 15.9 percent from 1990. At the same time Port Washington's male unemployed decreased by 34.7 percent, while females decreased by 17.9 percent.

Significant is that between 1990 and 2000 Port Washington's unemployment had fallen slightly less than two times Nassau County's decrease. Also important was that Port Washington's workforce contracted nearly twice Nassau County's, and that Port Washington's 2000 male unemployed fell more than 2 times the decrease of Nassau County's male unemployed.

A comparison between employed and unemployed reveals how Port Washington had fared as compared to Nassau County. Between 1990 and 2000, the ratio of the 30,298 decreases in employment in the Nassau County economy for those 16 years of age and older, to the drop of 4,405 in unemployed was 6.88 to 1. Port Washington's ratio of the 1,359-employment loss to decrease in unemployment was 8.0 to 1. In 1990, the Nassau County ratio was 23.2 persons employed to every person unemployed, with a 25.6 to 1 ratio in Port Washington. By 2000, the Nassau County ratio improved to 26.1 to 1, while Port Washington grew to 32.4 to 1. Port Washington had become an economic entity unto itself, clearly reacting favorably to the global economy, while also contributing to the regional economy, with median family and per capita income exceeding that of the surrounding Nassau County.

FAMILY INCOME:
The socioeconomic infrastructure of Port Washington continued to improve. Residents kept pace or exceeded Nassau County in academic attainment and job skills, with Port Washington workers having the required skills necessary for higher paying jobs created regionally by the global economy. The result was a workforce capable of entrepreneurship and of accessing the higher paying jobs being created by the regional economy, Tables 10 and 11 reflect how family income in Port Washington improved between 1990 and 2000, and continued to exceed income growth for Nassau County.

Table 10: Nominal Family Income

Nominal Family Income	Nassau County Families (a)		Port Washington Families (b)	
	1990			
$0 - $5,000	4,247	1.2%	65	.8%
$5,000-$9,999	4,733	1.4%	142	1.8%
$10,000-$14,999	7,557	2.2%	133	1.7%
$15,000-$24,999	24,082	6.9%	617	8.0%
$25,000-$49,999	89,077	25.7%	1,586	20.5%
$50,000 and over	217,094	62.6%	5,215	67.2%
Total	346,790	100%	7,758	100%
	2000			
Nominal Family Income	**Nassau County Families (a)**		**Port Washington Families (b)**	
$0-$9,999	7,572	2.2%	251	3.2%
$10,000-$14,999	6,066	1.7%	102	1.3%
$15,000-$24,999	16,312	4.7%	283	3.6%
$25,000-$49,999	57,426	16.4%	1,052	13.5%
$50,000 and over	262,318	75.0%	6,111	78.4%
Total	349,694	100%	7,799	100%

Source: (a) 1990 U.S. Census Table DP-4, Income and Poverty Status in 1989; 2000 U.S. Census Table DP-3, Profile of Selected Economic Characteristics: 2000.

(b) Infoshare.org. 1990 U.S. Census Table: Family Income in 1989; 2000 U.S. Census Table: Family Income in 1999.

CHAPTER VI

In 1990, the 4.3 percent of Port Washington families represented at the lower income categories was slightly lower than the 4.8 percent of Nassau County families earning $15,000 or less. Port Washington families earning over $25,000 were comparable to Nassau County families, while 67.2 percent of Port Washington families earned over $50,000, as compared to 62.6 percent of Nassau County families. By 2000, correlating with the improving educational attainment, economic conditions continued to improve to where only 3.9 percent of Nassau County families and 4.5 percent of Port Washington families were earning less than $15,000. Furthermore, 91.4 percent of Nassau County families earned in excess of $25,000, exceeded by 91.9 percent of Port Washington families. In part because more residents attended or graduated college, Nassau County families earning over $50,000 improved from 62.6 percent in 1990 to 75.0 percent in 2000, with the gap between those earning over $100,000 annually also narrowing. In 1990, the 19.6 percent of Nassau County families earning over $100,000 was 57 percent of the corresponding 34.1 percent of Port Washington families. By 2000, Nassau County families earning over $100,000, nearly doubling to 37.4 percent, was now 73 percent of the corresponding 51 percent of Port Washington families earning over $100,000, a 28 percent increase from 1990. Reflecting a higher percent of college attendees and graduates, Port Washington families earning over $50,000 per year improved from 67.2 percent in 1990 to 78.4 percent by 2000. Indicative of the higher earnings of the Port Washington workforce are differences in mean per capita and family median income between Nassau County and Port Washington, and are presented in Table 11.

Table 11 Mean Per Capita and Median Family (Nominal and Real) Income

| | | 1990 | | 2000 | |
		Mean Per Capita	Median Family	Mean Per Capita	Median Family
Nassau	Nominal $	$23,352	$60,619	$32,151	$81,246
County: (a)	Real $ (1)	$16,873	$43,800	$17,588	$44,445
Port	Nominal $	$32,024	$72,279	$47,448	$102,064
Washington:	Real $ (1)	$23,139	$52,225	$25,956	$55,833
(b)					

Source: (a) 1990 U.S. Census Table DP-4, 2000 U.S. Census Table DP-3.
  (b) Infoshare.org, 1990 U.S. Census Tables: Median Family Income in 1989 and Per Capita Income in 1989; 2000 U.S. Census Tables: Median Family Income in 1999 and Per Capita Income in 1999.
Note (1): Based on 1984 CPI as the base year, New York Area Index as of July 1990 and July 2000.

The 1990 Port Washington mean per capita and median family incomes, expressed in both nominal and real dollars, were respectively 137 and 119 percent of their Nassau County equivalents. This gap widened by 2000, with the Nassau County nominal mean per capita and median family incomes experiencing a respective 38 and 34 percent growth between 1990 and 2000, while mean per capita and median incomes expressed in real dollars grew by 4.2 and 1.5 percent respectively. Exceeding Nassau County, the growth of Port Washington's mean per capita and median family incomes expressed in nominal dollars grew by 48.2 and 41.2 percent, with mean per capita and median income expressed in real dollars increasing by 12.2 and 6.9 percent respectively. The Port Washington mean per capita and median family incomes expressed in both nominal and real dollars had now increased to 147 and 125 percent of their Nassau County equivalents. Not only had Port Washington kept up with Nassau County, but it actually gained economic ground, another indication of prospering in the global economy.

HOUSING:

As would be expected, with the additional costs of home ownership, including down payment requirements, the higher mean per capita and median family incomes in Port Washington should have had a positive impact on the incidence of home ownership. However, as compared to Nassau County in Table 12, that was not the case.

Table 12: Occupied Housing Units

		1990		2000		Increase (Decrease)	
Nassau	Total occupied units	431,515	100%	447,387	100%	15,872	3.7%
County:	Owner occupied	347,143	80.4%	359,264	80.3%	12,121	3.5%
(a)	Renter occupied	84,372	19.6%	88,123	19.7%	3,751	4.4%
Port	Total occupied units	10,246	100%	10,454	100%	208	2.0%
Washington:	Owner occupied	6,792	66.3%	6,942	66.4%	150	2.2%
(b)	Renter occupied	3,454	33.7%	3,512	33.6%	58	1.7%

Source: (a) 1990 U.S. Census Table DP-1, 2000 U.S. Census Tables DP-1.
 (b) Infoshare.org, 1990 U.S. Census Table: Tenure (owner/renter); 2000 U.S. Census Table: owner/renter.

In 1990, of the total occupied housing units in Nassau County, 80.4 percent were owner occupied and 19.6 percent renter occupied. Of Port Washington's 1990 total occupied housing units, 66.3 percent were owner occupied with 33.7 percent renter occupied. By 2000, total Nassau County housing units had increased by 3.7 percent, with 76 percent of the increase owner occupied units, and 24 percent renter occupied. In Port Washington, the total occupied housing units increased by 2.0 percent, with 72 percent of the increase owner occupied units, and 28 percent renter occupied. Nassau County experienced a respective 3.5 and 4.4 percent balanced increase in owner and renter occupied housing units, as did Port Washington with a 2.2 and 1.7 percent respective increases in owner and renter occupied housing units. While more owner occupied units of housing were built, Nassau County's percent growth in owner occupied housing units had lagged 25 percent behind that of renter occupied units, while in Port Washington the percent of owner-occupied housing units grew 25 percent faster than renter-occupied units.

In a trend that continued between 1990 and 2000, the 1990 median gross rent in Port Washington of $934, was 38 percent more than the Nassau County median gross rent of $678. By 2000, the median gross rent of Port Washington had increased 41 percent to $1,316, as compared to the 42 percent increase in Nassau County's median gross rent of $964.[50] Interestingly, in line with higher incomes, renters in Port Washington paid 36 percent more in rent than Nassau County as a whole.

---

[50] Source: For Nassau County: 1990 U.S. Census, table DP-1, 2000 U.S. Census table DP-4. For Port Washington: Infoshare.org; 1990 U.S. Census Table; Median Gross Rent; 2000 U.S. Census Table: Median Gross Rent.

CHAPTER VI
SUMMARY:

The Port Washington socioeconomic indicators of family structure, academic attainment, workforce participation, jobs skills, household income, and home ownership, were at more favorable levels as compared to Nassau County as a whole. During the decade of the 1990's, in comparison to the surrounding Nassau County, Port Washington has:

(1)   had a shrinking of its African-American community and growth in other minorities, while experiencing population growth at one-third the rate of Nassau County;

(2)   experienced an increase in families with a male and female present, and had more families headed by women than men;

(3)   had a strengthening of traditional family structure, where there are fewer single males and females as compared to married males and females;

(4)   had slower growth in college enrollments, with greater student enrollment in elementary and high school;

(5)   comparable growth in post-secondary education attainment, but with Port Washington pulling ahead in higher education, widening an already existing higher education attainment gap with Nassau County;

(6)   had a dramatic increase in self-employed entrepreneurs, a significant decrease in private sector employment, and an increase government employment;

(7)   similar to Nassau County, had losses in higher paying professional and managerial and administrative jobs, yet had dramatic increases in lower paying service, clerical, and sales jobs;

(8)   experienced decreases in male and female employed, with sharper decreases in both male and female unemployment;

(9)   had growth in nominal median family and mean per capita income, 78.4 percent of families earning nominal income above $50,000 as compared to 75 percent of Nassau County families;

(10)   had nominal mean per capita and median family income grow at a faster rate than Nassau County's, with increases in Port Washington's real mean per capita and median family income;

(11)   had a modest increase in owner and renter occupied housing units with renter occupied units remaining 33 percent of total occupied units; while modest growth was also experienced in Nassau County, renter occupied units were less than 20 percent of occupied units in Nassau County.

Overall, the growth experienced by Port Washington between 1990 and 2000 not only kept pace with surrounding Nassau County, but also in many instances out performed the region.

What appears too obvious to ignore is how a white community out performed three communities of color is so many socio-economic indicators. This begs the question as to what influence institutional racism plays in the presented data and analysis and what added benefit or burden race plays in the access to the opportunities and education so relevant and necessary to succeed in the global economy.

The one consistency in communities that have adapted to the changes brought by the global economy and the deindustrialization of the Long Island region has been the level entrepreneurship in the local employment base. Port Washington, a primarily white, well-educated community, has a greater proportion of self-employed in its employment base than Nassau County taken as a whole, and the communities of color of Roosevelt, North Amityville, and Huntington Station. While the struggle of minority entrepreneurs is well documented, and appears in the data for North Amityville, Huntington Station and Roosevelt, their ability to adapt to the regional economy has been made more complicated by the global economy, and barriers imposed by institutional racism. Those challenges are illustrated in the following analysis.

CHAPTER VI

Chapter VII

SUFFOLK COUNTY
MINORITY ENTREPRENEURSHIP:
ADAPTING TO THE GLOBAL ECONOMY

A key element to entrepreneurship is that successful evaluation of business risks is rewarded by the profits that ensue. That is what drives entrepreneurs. The global economy however, has added a new perspective to successful entrepreneurship.

During the last century, emerging entrepreneurs only required a domestic view of business to appraise the business risk and profit equation. That is to assess regional and national differences in manufacturing and labor costs, costs and availability of capital, and the markets where their goods and services would be sold. Today, the global economy alters that equation.

The current global economic climate is different, and is based on changes in technology and communications, strongly influenced by international and interdependent capital flows, commodity markets, information, raw materials, management and organization, where information transfers happen instantaneously. Contemporary and emerging entrepreneurs have to recognize, understand, and adapt to these external influences. The basic business risk and profit equation has not changed; it is the elements included in the equation that have become more complex due to the ramifications of global markets.

Fundamentals of the Global Economy: Impact on Entrepreneurship

As entrepreneurs who preceded them, the current generation of entrepreneurs have more challenges to overcome in this new economic order, which has been made more difficult by technological advances, which now favor intellectual over physical attributes. This has effectively transferred skills once provided by workers to machines; blue-collar, manufacturing jobs, once epitomized by the assembly line, now have been replaced by computers with their attendant technical and professional personnel. As noted earlier, further complicating emerging entrepreneurship is evident in what can be called the global assembly line, where production and assembly of goods originate from factories and depots throughout the world wherever labor costs and economies of scale make an international division of labor cost-effective. The globalization of production and assembly has created the need for increased centralization and complexity of management, control, and planning. The complexity of participating in world markets and foreign countries has resulted in diversification of product lines, mergers, and transnationalization of economic activities that require highly specialized skills in top-level management. This has fostered growth and development of higher levels of expertise among producer service firms such as accountants, attorneys, programmers, and financial, banking, public relations and management consultants, now being asked to improve upon their support services to where they now become crucial elements in corporate and entrepreneurship decision making. Thus, emerging entrepreneurs must understand the multinational company with whom they are now competing; including dispersed manufacturing facilities, which contribute to the development of new type of planning and distribution required for its business.[51] A good example of the challenges confronting Long Island employees is the recent announcement by *Newsday* that it is relocating 50 consumer servicing jobs to the Pacific Rim, costing Long Islanders their livelihoods. *Newsday's* parent company is seeking to find savings in the lower payroll cost available in Asia. This is a classic example of the economic challenges confronting domestic companies in a global economy.

While geographically Long Island, and in particular Suffolk County's minority communities, may be considered to be on the perimeter of the centers of global activity, the proximity to New York City, considered a leading global city, has impacted the Long Island region. The growth of Long Island's finance and banking sectors as well as the presence of many multi-national companies has brought the impact and complexity of the global economy to the region.

At the same time that changes in technology were producing new jobs and creating new entrepreneurship opportunities, they were also making others obsolete. The technologically revolutionized workplace was widening the gap between skilled and unskilled workers, and higher and lower paying jobs, primarily because education and training had grown to become more important then ever.

While there has been improvement in educational attainment in many Suffolk County minority communities, the emergence of entrepreneurs in these communities, as has been shown in North Amityville, Huntington Station and Roosevelt, has been hampered because of the lack of networking opportunities, lack of access to the mainstream business community, low levels of education in the community workforce, and unskilled workers tending to be out of work or poorly paid. These results are unlike the significant entrepreneurial growth in primarily White Port Washington.

The interaction between technological and international competition demanded by the global economy has eroded the basic institutions of the mass production system, which has now become reliant on productivity improvements where human capital costs have been replaced by technology and the few educated professional, technical, and managerial workers necessary for production.[52] The service delivery system has been similarly impacted, as with the case of *Newsday*, which is not alone in the shifting of domestic customer service centers to the lower wage Pacific Rim nations.

Adapting to these significant structural changes in international commerce is complex enough for companies able to access the necessary professional advisory services. For minority entrepreneurs operating with low capitalization, and striving to overcome institutional racism, it is financially overwhelming and at times impossible to achieve.

How entrepreneurs in Suffolk County, and in particular nine of its most culturally and ethnically diverse African-American, Hispanic and White communities fared between 1990 and 2000 are presented in the following analysis.

Reviewed will be how this period of industrial and economic restructuring impacted Suffolk County's minority entrepreneurs. Would minority entrepreneurs be able to achieve parity with their white counterparts? Would the global economy impact the emergence of minority entrepreneurs? Would there be an entrepreneurship gap between communities of color and white communities?

The answers to these questions are found in the following comparison between nine

---

[51] Saskia Sassen, (Princeton: Princeton University Press, 1991), p. 10-11.
[52] Ibid, p. 151.

multi-cultural African-American, Hispanic, and White communities, with the surrounding primarily white, and economically more prosperous Suffolk County.

Suffolk County Entrepreneurship: What's Race Got To Do With It.

With the perspective of the changes, pressures, and impact on the Long Island economy and industry sectors caused by the global economy, Table A presents the existence of an entrepreneurship gap in Suffolk County, and in particular Tables 1 through 9in the communities of color such as North Amityville; North Bellport; Brentwood; Central Islip; Flanders, Riverside, Hampton Bays and Pine Valley; Gordon Heights; Huntington Station; Riverhead; and Wyandanch.

Table A: Entreneurship Gap: Suffolk County Entrepreneuship By Race

	Total Employed	% of Total Employed	Self-Employed	% of Total Employed	% of Total Self-Employed	% of Race
Suffolk County Self-employed Population for Employed Civilian Population over 16 Years Old by Race (2000)						
White Alone (Not Hispanic or Latino)	550,600	80.6%	61,779	9.0%	87.8%	11.2%
Black or African American Alone and Combined with Other Races (Not Hispanic or Latino)	41,304	6.0%	1,674	0.2%	2.4%	4.0%
Hispanic or Latino (Any Race)	67,411	9.9%	4,556	0.7%	6.5%	6.8%
Other	23,747	3.5%	2,369	0.4%	3.3%	9.9%
Total Employed	683,062	100.0%	70,378	10.3%	100.0%	-

**Source: 2000 Census, Summary File 4, Table PCT87

According to the 2000 Census the majority of the employed civilian population are White Alone. 80.6% of the total 683,062-employed population is White Alone (Not Hispanic) followed by Hispanic or Latino of any race at 9.9%, Black or African American Alone and Combined with Other Races (Not Hispanic or Latino) with 6.0% and other racial categories which were classified as Other representing 3.5%.

The total employed civilian population over 16 years old, was disproportionately weighted towards the White Alone category representing 550,600 persons or 80.6 of those employed in Suffolk County and 9.0% of the total self-employed population. Whites Alone are the highest percentage self-employed when compared to the 683,062 employed in Suffolk County. The 61,779 Whites Alone that are self-employed overshadow the second highest classification, Hispanic or Latino, which represent .7% of the self-employed population. Those classified as Other represent .2% while Black or African American Alone with Other Races (Not Hispanic or Latino) represent .4%.

Further analysis of self-employment in Suffolk County revealed that those identified as self-employed White Alone, represent the highest percentage self-employed in Suffolk County with 87.8%. The second highest racial classification regarding self-employment as compared against the total self-employed in Suffolk County is Hispanic or Latinos with 6.5%. They are followed by those classified as Other with 3.3% and Black or African American Alone and Combined Races (Not Hispanic or Latino) with 2.4%.

When reviewing how each group's self-employment compared to their own rates of employment in the civilian population over 16 years of Age, there is slightly less disparity. Whites Alone still represent the highest percentage, with 11.2%, of their overall employed population. They are followed by those classified as Other with 9.9%, Latino or Hispanics with 6.8% and Blacks or African Americans with 4.0%.

Conclusion:

- 10.3% of the employed population in Suffolk County is classified as Self-Employed.

- Those classified as Whites Alone in Suffolk County substantially and disproportionately exceeded all other groups classified as Employed.

- Minorities substantially lagged behind Whites with regard to the percent of self-employed when compared to the total employed population, the self-employed population, and to each group's individual amount of self-employed workers, with Hispanics faring better than Blacks. This glaring minority entrepreneurship gap in Suffolk is defined in further detail in the following nine Suffolk County communities of color.

Table 1: North Amityville:

North Amityville Self-employed Population for Employed Civilian Population over 16 Years Old by Race (2000)						
	Total Employed	% of Total Employed	Self-Employed	% of Total Employed	% of Total Self-Employed	% of Race
White Alone (Not Hispanic or Latino)	913	13.4%	64	0.9%	22.6%	7.0%
Black or African American Alone and Combined with Other Races (Not Hispanic or Latino)	4,983	73.1%	181	2.7%	64.0%	3.6%
Hispanic or Latino (Any Race)	745	10.9%	8	0.1%	2.8%	1.1%
Other	179	2.6%	30	0.4%	10.6%	16.8%
Total Employed	6,820	100.0%	283	4.1%	100.0%	-

**Source: 2000 Census, Summary File 4, Table PCT87

The North Amityville study area encompassed Census Tracts: 1232.02, 1233.01, and 1233.02. Unlike the Suffolk County findings, the Black or African American classification represents a higher percentage of those employed in this study area with 4,983 or 73.1%. White Alone follows with 13.4% of the total 6,820-employed population, and then Hispanic or Latino of any race, and those classified as Other representing 10.9% and 2.6% respectively.

When looking at these racial classifications as they pertain to the employed civilian population over 16 years old, we again see a divergence when compared to Suffolk County as a whole. Blacks or African Americans represent the highest percentage of the total self-employed with 181 people or 2.7% of the overall 4.1% or 283 people that comprise the total amount of self-employed in North Amityville. Those classified as White Alone follows with .9%, then Other representing 0.6%, and Hispanic or Latino with .1% self-employed.

Looking deeper at the issue of self-employment in North Amityville we examined the individual rates of self-employment as compared with the total amount of self-employed for each racial classification. Those identified as self-employed Black or African American represent the highest percentage self-employed with 64.0%. The second highest racial classification regarding self-employment as compared against the total self-employed population in North Amityville is White Alone with 22.6%. They are followed by those classified as Other with 10.6% and Hispanic or Latino with 2.8%.

When assessing how each groups' self-employment rates perform when compared to their own rates of employment for the civilian population over 16 years of Age, what is clear is that the 16.8 % of those classified as Other represent the highest percentage of their category as self-employed. However we also must note that they are also the lowest frequency of the total employed. An interesting point, when looking at the other categories, Whites Alone still represent the highest percentage, with 7.0%, of their overall employed population, despite being only 13.4% of the total employed. They are followed by those classified as Black or African American with 3.6%, despite, representing 73.1% of the total employed, and the highest percentage of those employed.

Conclusion:

- Although, Blacks or African American make up the majority of those employed and those self-employed, when compared to the self-employment totals for themselves as a racial group, their self-employment rate lags far behind both White Alone and Other by 51.4% and 21.4 % respectively.

Table 2: North Bellport:

North Bellport Self-employed Population for Employed Civilian Population over 16 Years Old by Race (2000)						
	Total Employed	% of Total Employed	Self-Employed	% of Total Employed	% of Total Self-Employed	% of Race
White Alone (Not Hispanic or Latino)	579	33.1%	46	2.7%	52.9%	7.9%
Black or African American Alone and Combined with Other Races (Not Hispanic or Latino)	690	39.4%	11	0.6%	12.6%	1.6%
Hispanic or Latino (Any Race)	414	23.7%	30	1.7%	34.5%	7.2%
Other	66	3.8%	0	0.0%	0.0%	0.0%
Total Employed	1,749	100.0%	87	5.0%	100.0%	-

**Source: 2000 Census, Summary File 4, Table PCT87

Represented by Census Tract: 1591.03, North Bellport employment is characterized by Blacks or African Americans having the highest employment percentages with 690 people or 39.4% out of the total of 1,749 employed. They are followed by 579 White Alone at 33.1% of the total, then by 414 Hispanic or Latino of any race representing

23.7%, and then by those classified as Other, having the lowest percentage of employed with 66 persons or 3.8%.

When looking at the racial classifications of the employed civilian population over 16 years old, although Blacks or African Americans make up the highest percentage of those employed, they represent the lowest percentage of self-employed in North Bellport with a rate of 0.6% of the total self-employed. Whites Alone, lagging behind Blacks in percentage of employed, have the highest percentage self-employed when compared to the total amount of employed with 2.7%, followed by Hispanic or Latino with 1.7%.

Further review of self-employment in North Bellport, as compared with the total amount of self-employed for each racial classification reveals that those identified as self-employed White Alone represent the highest percentage self-employed with 52.9%. The second highest racial classification regarding self-employment, as compared against the total self-employed are Hispanic or Latinos with 34.5%. They are followed by those classified as Black or African American Alone and Combined Races (Not Hispanic or Latino) with 12.6%.

When looking at how each groups' self-employment rates perform when compared to their own rates of employment for the civilian population over 16 years of Age, we once again find White Alone representing the highest percentage, with 7.9%, of their overall employed population. They are again followed by Latino or Hispanics with 7.2% of self-employed and Blacks or African Americans with 1.6%.

Conclusion:

- Despite North Bellport Blacks and African Americans exceeding Whites with regard to those employed, and with Hispanic or Latinos slightly lagging behind both groups, Whites fair better than both Blacks or African Americans and Hispanic or Latinos with regards to self-employment rates.

- Furthermore, when self-employed Black or African Americans are measured against both the total self-employed and the total of employed Blacks, they substantially lag behind both Hispanics and Others.

CHAPTER VII

Table 3: Brentwood:

Brentwood **Self-employed Population for Employed Civilian Population over 16 Years Old by Race** **(2000)**						
	Total Employed	**% of Total Employed**	**Self-Employed**	**% of Total Employed**	**% of Total Self-Employed**	**% of Race**
White Alone (Not Hispanic or Latino)	1,069	14.4%	21	0.3%	8.9%	2.0%
Black or African American Alone and Combined with Other Races (Not Hispanic or Latino)	899	12.1%	29	0.4%	12.2%	3.2%
Hispanic or Latino (Any Race)	4,957	66.8%	155	2.1%	65.4%	3.1%
Other	499	6.7%	32	0.4%	13.5%	6.4%
Total Employed	7,424	100.0%	237	3.2%	100.0%	-

**Source: 2000 Census, Summary File 4, Table PCT87

The boundaries of Brentwood are defined by Census Tracts: 1456.03, 1456.04, 1460.01, and 1461.04. According to the 2000 Census, the majority of the total employed are Hispanic or Latino, representing 66.8% of the total 7,424 persons, followed by 14.4% of White Alone, 12.1% of Black or African American Alone and Combined with Other Races (Not Hispanic or Latino), and 6.7% of other racial categories which are classified as Other.

The racial composition of Brentwood's self-employed, when compared to the total employed reflects the highest percentage for Hispanic or Latinos of 2.1%. The Other category, although representing the fewest amount of people in the workforce are the second highest percentage of self-employed with 0.4%. Those classified as Black or African American Alone with Other Races (Not Hispanic or Latino) follow with 0.4% with White Alone at 0.3%.

Further analysis of self-employment in Brentwood finds that of those identified as self-employed Hispanic or Latino, represent the highest percentage self-employed with 65.4%. The second highest racial classification of self-employment, as compared to the total self-employed is Other with 13.5%, followed by those classified as Black or African American Alone and Combined Races (Not Hispanic or Latino) with 12.2% and White Alone with 8.9%. Despite 'Other" having 6.7% of the Brentwood employment over 16 years old, Other self-employed represents the highest percentage of their individual population, with 6.4%, followed by Black and African Americans with 3.2%, Latino or Hispanics with 3.1% and Whites with 2.0%.

Conclusion:

- Blacks or African Americans and Hispanic or Latinos have higher self-employment rates than Whites in all categories of self-employment. This despite White employed and self-employed participating more in the overall Suffolk County employment base.

Table 4: Central Islip:

	Total Employed	% of Total Employed	Self-Employed	% of Total Employed	% of Total Self-Employed	% of Race
Central Islip _Self-employed Population for Employed Civilian Population over 16 Years Old by Race (2000)_						
White Alone (Not Hispanic or Latino)	2,065	37.6%	89	1.6%	55.3%	4.3%
Black or African American Alone and Combined with Other Races (Not Hispanic or Latino)	1,280	23.3%	11	0.2%	6.8%	0.9%
Hispanic or Latino (Any Race)	1,872	34.1%	54	1.0%	33.5%	2.9%
Other	277	5.0%	7	0.1%	4.4%	2.5%
Total Employed	5,494	100.0%	161	2.9%	100.0%	-

**Source: 2000 Census, Summary File 4, Table PCT87

Census Tracts: 1457.04 and 1462.03 define the boundaries of the Central Islip study area. 37.6% of the total 5,494 employed are White Alone (Not Hispanic), followed by Hispanic or Latino of any race with 34.1%, then by Black or African American Alone and Combined with Other Races (Not Hispanic or Latino) with 23.3%, with the remaining 5% comprised of other racial categories classified as Other.

The relationship of the aggregate of racial classifications to the employed civilian population over 16 years old reflects a relatively 2.9 percent of self-employed within this study area. Of that low number of 161 self-employed, the highest amount of self-employed, as compared to the total employed, are White Alone with 1.6%. Hispanic or Latino, Black or African America, and Other follow them with 1.0%, 0.2% and 0.1% respectively.

Investigating further the issue of self-employment in Central Islip, we examined the rates of self-employment as compared with the total of self-employed for each racial classification. Those identified as White Alone represent the highest percentage self-employed with 55.3% or 89 people. The second highest racial classifications regarding self-employment as compared to the total self-employed population in Central Islip are Hispanic or

Latinos with 33.5%. They are followed by Black or African American Alone and Combined Races (Not Hispanic or Latino) with 6.8% and Other with 4.4%

When looking at how each groups' self-employment rates perform when compared to their own rates of employment for the civilian population over 16 years of Age, slightly less stratified percentages result. Whites Alone still represent the highest percentage, with 4.3%%, of their overall employed population. They are followed by those classified as Hispanic or Latino with 2.9%, Other with 2.5% and Blacks or African Americans with 0.9%.

Conclusion:

- Although Whites in the employed population represent a slightly larger percentage than both Hispanics or Latinos and Black or African Americans, they exceed Hispanics or Latinos by 65.1% and African American or Blacks by 713% when compared to the overall percentage of those self-employed in the Central Islip Community.

- When compared to each own racial group, Whites represent a higher percentage of self-employment than any other racial classification.

Table 5: Flanders, Hampton Bays, Pine Valley, and Riverside:

Flanders, Hampton Bays, Pine Valley, Riverside Self-employed Population for Employed Civilian Population over 16 Years Old by Race (2000)						
	Total Employed	**% of Total Employed**	**Self-Employed**	**% of Total Employed**	**% of Total Self-Employed**	**% of Race**
White Alone (Not Hispanic or Latino)	1,891	65.6%	235	8.2%	80.5%	12.4%
Black or African American Alone and Combined with Other Races (Not Hispanic or Latino)	680	23.6%	2	0.1%	0.7%	0.3%
Hispanic or Latino (Any Race)	214	7.4%	32	1.1%	10.9%	14.9%
Other	96	3.4%	23	0.8%	7.9%	23.9%
Total Employed	2,881	100.0%	292	10.2%	100.0%	-

**Source: 2000 Census, Summary File 4, Table PCT87

The boundary for the Flanders, Hampton Bays, Pinewood Valley, and Riverside study area is Census Tract: 1904.01. Within this boundary we see the White Alone classification as having the highest percentage of those employed with 65.6%. They are followed by the 23.6% of Black or African Americans, Hispanic or Latino with 7.4%, and other racial categories, classified as Other with 3.4%.

When assessing these racial classifications as compared to the employed civilian population over 16 years old, we again see a disproportionately high amount of the White Alone category representing 8.2% of the total employed people in the study area. The second highest classification is Hispanic or Latino, which represents 1.1% of the self-employed population when compared to the total employed population. Those classified as Other represent 0.8% while Black or African American Alone with Other Races (Not Hispanic or Latino) represent .1%.

Further analysis of self-employment in Flanders, Hampton Bays, Pinewood Valley, and Riverside finds that those identified as self-employed White Alone, represent the highest percentage self-employed in the study area with 80.5%. Following are Hispanic or Latinos with 10.9%, then those classified as Other and Blacks or African American with 7.9% and 0.7% respectively.

Reviewing how these groups' self-employment rates compare to their own rates of employment for the civilian population over 16 years old, those classified as Other are fewest in number, yet they report the highest percentage of those employed in their category with 23.9%. They are followed by those classified as Latino or Hispanics with 14.9%, White Alone with 12.4% despite being the second highest group in terms of employment, and Blacks or African Americans with 0.3%.

Conclusion:

- Hispanic or Latinos have the third lowest percentage of employment in this study area. However, when measuring the self-employed against Hispanic employment they have the second highest self-employment rate at 14.9% after those classified as others.

- Black or African Americans have the lowest rate of self-employment in all measures.

Table 6: Gordon Heights:

	Gordon Heights Self-employed Population for Employed Civilian Population over 16 Years Old by Race (2000)					
	Total Employed	% of Total Employed	Self-Employed	% of Total Employed	% of Total Self-Employed	% of Race
White Alone (Not Hispanic or Latino)	315	24.5%	30	2.3%	46.1%	9.5%
Black or African American Alone and Combined with Other Races (Not Hispanic or Latino)	747	58.0%	25	1.9%	38.5%	3.3%
Hispanic or Latino (Any Race)	173	13.4%	0	0.0%	0.0%	0.0%
Other	53	4.1%	10	0.8%	15.4%	18.9%
Total Employed	1,288	100.0%	65	5.0%	100.0%	-

**Source: 2000 Census, Summary File 4, Table PCT87

The Boundaries for the Gordon Heights study area is Census Tract, 1587.05. 58% of the total 1,288 employed population are Black of African American Alone and Combined with Other Races (Not Hispanic or Latino), followed by the 24.5% of White Alone, Hispanic or Latino (Any Race) with 13.4% and other racial categories classified as Other at 4.1%. Despite Blacks and African Americans exceeding Whites with the largest employment rate, they represented only 1.9% of Gordon Heights self-employed, lagging behind White Alone at 2.3%.

When examining the rates of self-employment as compared with the total amount of self-employed, White Alone represents the highest percentage self-employed, in Gordon Heights with 46.1%. Following were Black or African Americans with 38.5% and those classified as Other with 15.4%.

When looking at how each groups' self-employment rates compared to their own rates of employment for the civilian population over 16 years of Age, Other represented the highest percentage with 18.9%, followed by those classified as White Alone with 9.5%, and by Blacks or African Americans with 3.3%.

Conclusion:

- Blacks or African Americans have the greatest amount of employed people and the highest employment rate. However, they have lower percentages of self-employment, by all measures, when compared to Whites.

Table 7: Huntington Station:

	Total Employed	% of Total Employed	Self-Employed	% of Total Employed	% of Total Self-Employed	% of Race
Huntington Station Self-employed Population for Employed Civilian Population over 16 Years Old by Race (2000)						
White Alone (Not Hispanic or Latino)	9,685	65.4%	764	5.2%	71.5%	7.9%
Black or African American Alone and Combined with Other Races (Not Hispanic or Latino)	1,396	9.4%	34	0.2%	3.2%	2.4%
Hispanic or Latino (Any Race)	3,012	20.4%	204	1.4%	19.1%	6.8%
Other	714	4.8%	66	0.4%	6.2%	9.2%
Total Employed	14,807	100.0%	1,068	7.2%	100.0%	-

**Source: 2000 Census, Summary Table 4, Table PCT87

The jurisdictional boundaries of the Huntington Station CDP were used to determine the Huntington Station study area. Those classified as White Alone comprise 65.4% of the total 14,807 employed, followed by Hispanic or Latino represent 20.4% of the total employed, 9.4% of Black or African Americans, and Other Races comprising 4.8%.

When each racial classification is compared to the employed civilian population over 16 years old, we find a high amount of the White Alone category representing 5.2% of self-employed. The 9,685 Whites Alone that are self-employed substantially exceeded the second highest classification, Hispanic or Latino, which represented 1.4% of the self-employed when compared to the total employed. Those classified as Other represent 0.4% while Black or African American Alone with Other Races (Not Hispanic or Latino) represent 0.2%.

When comparisons are made between self-employed in Huntington Station and those identified as self-employed, White Alone represented the highest percentage of self-employed with 71.5%. The second highest racial classification of self-employment as compared against the total self-employed is Hispanic or Latinos with 19.1%. They are followed by those classified as Other with 6.2% and Black or African American Alone and Combined Races (Not Hispanic or Latino) with 3.2%.

When evaluating how each groups' self-employment rates perform when compared to their own rates of employment for the civilian population over 16 years of Age, we found that those classified as Other represented 9.2% of its self-employed. They were followed by those classified as White Alone with 7.9%, Latino or Hispanics with 6.8% and Blacks or African Americans with 2.4%.

CHAPTER VII

Conclusion:

- Unlike other minority communities, there is a symmetrical distribution of self-employed between the racial components similar to their racial composition in Huntington Station. Both Blacks or African Americans and Hispanic or Latinos lag behind Whites in all measures of self-employment.

Table 8: Riverhead:

	Total Employed	% of Total Employed	Self-Employed	% of Total Employed	% of Total Self-Employed	% of Race
Riverhead Self-employed Population for Employed Civilian Population over 16 Years Old by Race (2000)						
White Alone (Not Hispanic or Latino)	2,798	65.1%	412	9.6%	85.3%	14.7%
Black or African American Alone and Combined with Other Races (Not Hispanic or Latino)	959	22.3%	58	1.3%	12.0%	6.0%
Hispanic or Latino (Any Race)	389	9.0%	13	0.3%	2.7%	3.3%
Other	155	3.6%	0	0.0%	0.0%	0.0%
Total Employed	4,301	100.0%	483	11.2%	100.0%	-

**Source: 2000 Census, Summary File 4, Table PCT87

The Riverhead CDP is used as the boundaries for the Riverhead Study Area. Within its boundaries, 65.1% of the total 4,301 employed are White Alone (Not Hispanic) followed by 22.3% of Black or African Americans, Hispanic or Latino with 9.0% and 3.6% other racial categories classified as Other.

When racial classifications are compared to the employed civilian population over 16 years old, we find a disproportionately high amount of the White Alone category representing 65.1% of employed people in Riverhead with self-employed representing 9.6% of total employed. White Alone are the highest percentage self-employed when compared to the total amount of employed people in the Study Area. The 2,798 Whites Alone that are self-employed substantially exceed the second highest classification, Black or African Americans that represent 22.3% of the total employed, with Black self-employed only 1.3% of total employment. Those classified as self-employed Hispanic or Latino represent 0.3% of total employed, while Others do not represent a statistically relevant amount of self-employed.

Further review of the self-employed, reveals that 85.3% identified as self-employed White Alone represent the highest percentage of Riverhead self-employed. The second highest racial classification of self-employment, as compared to the total self-employed are Black or African American with 12.0%, followed by those classified as Hispanic or Latino with 2.7%.

Following a similar pattern, when each racial group's self-employment rate, is compared to their own rates of employment for the civilian population over 16 years of Age, White Alone still represents the highest percentage with 14.7% of their overall employed population. They are followed by those classified as Black or African American with 6.0%, and Latino or Hispanics with 3.3%.

Conclusion:

- Whites in Riverhead reflect a majority of the employed population, percentage of total employed, percent of self-employed, and percent of self-employed in a racial classification.

- Both Blacks or African Americans and Hispanic or Latinos lag behind Whites by all measures of self-employment and total employment, with Blacks exceeding Hispanics.

Table 9: Wyandanch:

	Wyandanch Self-employed Population for Employed Civilian Population over 16 Years Old by Race (2000)					
	Total Employed	% of Total Employed	Self-Employed	% of Total Employed	% of Total Self-Employed	% of Race
White Alone (Not Hispanic or Latino)	105	2.6%	5	0.1%	3.1%	4.8%
Black or African American Alone and Combined with Other Races (Not Hispanic or Latino)	2,984	75.1%	119	3.0%	73.5%	4.0%
Hispanic or Latino (Any Race)	807	20.4%	38	1.0%	23.4%	4.7%
Other	76	1.9%	0	0.0%	0.0%	0.0%
Total Employed	3,972	100.0%	162	4.1%	100.0%	-

**Source: 2000 Census, Summary File 4, Table PCT87

The Jurisdictional boundaries of the Wyandanch CDP are used to determine the self-employment rates for the study area. According to the 2000 Census, 75.1% of the 3,972 total employed are Black or African American Alone and Combined with other Races (Not Hispanic or Latino), followed by 20.4% of Hispanic or Latino of any race, White Alone with 2.6%, and other racial categories classified as Other at 1.9%.

Analysis of the racial classifications as they pertain to the employed population over 16 years old, those classified as self-employed represent 4.1% of Wyandanch employed. Black self-employed represent 3% of total employed, followed by Hispanic or Latino representing 1%, and White Alone with 0.1%.

Further examination of self-employed finds that Black or African American represents the highest percentage self-employed people in Wyandanch with 73.5%, followed by Hispanic or Latinos with 23.4%, and White Alone with 3.1%.

Despite White Alone having the lowest employment rate and lowest percent of self-employed, they represent the highest percentage of self-employed of any racial category with 4.8% of White Alone employed. Hispanic or Latino follows them with 4.7%, and Blacks or African American with 4%.

Conclusion:

- Despite Black or African American representing the majority of those employed with in the study area, and having the highest percent of self-employed when measured against total self-employment, Blacks have lowest percent of self-employed among all racial groups in Wyandanch.

Summary: Suffolk County Minority Entrepreneurship

What is evident is that there is untapped economic potential in Long Island minority entrepreneurism as discussed in this report, and as presented in the following Table B.

- The racial distribution of White, Black, Hispanic and Other entrepreneurs in the local communities analyzed follows a distribution pattern similar to their racial composition of the Suffolk County employment base as a percent of race.

- Whites, regardless of their representation in the local community employment base, have a larger representative of entrepreneurs as a percent of their race.

- Other, which is primarily comprised of Asians, where they have representation in the local community employment base have a greater percentage of entrepreneurs as a percentage of their race.

- Hispanics or Latinos have a greater representation of entrepreneurs as a percentage of their race, in six of the nine profiled communities.

- Black entrepreneurs, as a percent of their racial component of the local community employment base lag behind all racial categories.

Table B: Comparison Of Self-Employed Percentage By Race (2000)

	Suffolk County	North Amityville	North Bellport	Brentwood	Central Islip	Flanders, Riverside, Hampton Bays	Gordon Heights	Huntington Station	Riverhead	Wyandanch
White (Not Hispanic or Latino)	11.2%	7.0%	7.9%	2.0%	4.3%	12.4%	9.5%	7.9%	14.7%	4.8%
Black or African American Alone and Combined with Other Races (Not Hispanic or Latino)	4.0%	3.6%	1.6%	3.2%	0.9%	0.3%	3.3%	2.4%	6.0%	4.0%
Hispanic or Latino (Any Race)	6.8%	1.1%	7.2%	3.1%	2.9%	14.9%	0.0%	6.8%	3.3%	4.7%
Other	9.9%	16.8%	0.0%	6.4%	2.5%	23.9%	18.9%	9.2%	0.0%	0.0%

CHAPTER VII

The analysis reveals that there may be untapped entrepreneurs in each of the presented communities, which indicates that there is growth potential in Suffolk County's entrepreneurial class, each representing a potential business. Experience indicates that providing incentives that not only encourage cultivation of Suffolk County minority entrepreneurs, but also concentrates their economic activity in their respective business district, will provide an important economic spark that can contribute to revitalizing their individual downtowns. As a critical mass of economic activity evolves, the downtown eventually becomes stronger than its individual parts. One way to accomplish this is with the creation of business and technology incubators in minority community business districts.

This is critical because the data indicates that a pattern of lagging minority entrepreneurial growth is becoming a permanent element of the regional economy. This at the very time that Long Island has been adjusting to the complexities of the technological requirements of the global economy.

Nurturing the development of minority entrepreneurs will provide residents in minority communities with the job opportunities to access the jobs that are being created in the Long Island economy.

Chapter VIII

EPILOGUE:
GLOBAL LONG ISLAND:
CONFRONTING THE 21ST CENTURY

What is clear from the previous analysis of North Amityville, Huntington Station, Roosevelt and Port Washington is that the global economy and a more diverse population have brought Long Island to an economic and sociological crossroad. The workforce is aging with the largest component, baby boomers nearing retirement age. The young people who would normally fill the vacated jobs are just over half the amount of projected retirees. To maintain the regional economy young people must sustain the workforce. However that future workforce is leaving Long Island for other lower cost regions of the country.

Housing is more expensive than young people can afford, and the dichotomy of the immigration issue has to be addressed-that of becoming a growing element of the Long Island workforce-while also requiring government intervention to provide safety, health services and education.

Energy costs, higher mortgage and consumer borrowing interest rates, and rising property taxes are becoming such a burden that they are becoming a drag on the regional job growth and expansion of the regional economy. To attract new property tax revenues, without creating sprawl to our open spaces, revitalization of downtowns, and Brownfield remediation are sensible alternatives. Reality of the marketplace dictates that more attention must be paid to Long Island's aging downtowns and Brownfield sites for mixed-use development opportunities. Both are ideal candidates for such efforts.

The public policy options that Long Island needs to address are inextricably intertwined with each other, with the resolution of each going a long way in deciding what Long Island, America's first suburb will look like in the 21st century.

Brownfields: Recycling Industrial Properties and Preserving Open Space

The economics of Brownfield redevelopment is the primary inhibitor to the effective use of these properties in revitalizing downtowns and becoming a source of affordable workforce housing necessary to keep young people on Long Island. The two most stubborn economic obstacles to Brownfields remediation are the cost and profitability associated with the cleanup, and the potential liability that accompanies the properties. When such properties are purchased at market rate, and then remediated, the total clean-up costs along with the insurance costs to cover liability, drives housing prices upward to cover these costs. To encourage Brownfields redevelopment, the costs of properties have to be lower, thus providing enough of an economic cushion to absorb the cost of clean up and to allow for a profit on development. Regulations have to be promulgated that confront local real estate market pressures that make these properties more expensive and cause the lack of participation by regional developers.

Brownfields remediation is so sensible because it addresses several needs. Environmentally, by recycling these properties, developers have alternatives to building on

Long Island's remaining parcels of open space, thus contributing to their preservation. There are incentives available to encourage housing construction, such as property density allowances, that will allow these once productive properties to be recycled. Thus contributing towards chipping away at Long Island's insatiable need for affordable housing, especially at the time when Long Island's opportunities for affordable housing are slipping away.

What is elusive are a workable set of regulations that accept the reality of the real estate market place and the cost of liability to those who wish to rehabilitate these properties.

Affordable Workforce Housing: Retaining Young People

Maintaining the vibrancy of the Long Island economy hinges on the availability of housing that young people can afford, since they will be the necessary replacement workers for the soon to retire baby boomers now in the workforce. Despite this apparent need, to achieve success the Long Island regional housing market must overcome two factors. The first is the conventional market factor of supply and demand, which is currently forcing home price increases to level out. The second are zoning code restrictions that regulate orderly housing growth. Often these two factors are compatible with each other, and with the economic and social fabric of a region. However this compatibility has not benefited lower income home purchasers. A recent study by the Joint Center for Housing Studies, the New York Metropolitan area, including Long Island is the 7th least affordable place to buy a home. Furthermore, New York State has the second highest percent of residents spending more than 50 percent of their incomes on housing.

Nonetheless, Long Island's real estate market is quickly pricing itself to where young people, and even potential buyers who have been working for several years, cannot afford a home. One factor causing this market dysfunction, which is unlikely to be reversed, is that potential homeowners have been earning wages whose growth has lagged behind the growth in local property taxes, energy costs and price increases of Long Island's housing stock.

Despite these factors, there continues to be activity in Long Island's home construction sector; with current home selling prices not increasing at the extent they once did. What has become obvious is that along with the leveling off of Long Island home selling prices, the inventory of houses for sale is increasing, with houses remaining on the market longer. A buyers market has now replaced the once strong regional sellers market.

With conventional market factors failing to adequately address the need for affordable housing, the practice of converting one-family homes into illegal two-family homes is growing. The result is that these illegal rentals congest Long Island neighborhoods with additional automobiles; overstresses residential sanitary systems and municipal services such as garbage removal; and increases student population in local school systems without a commensurate increase in school tax revenues.

The local Long Island debate focuses on the fact that illegal two-family homes create an inequity between those who follow the rules and pay their fare share of Long Island's high property taxes with those who don't. Furthermore, those that rent illegally more than likely take cash from their tenants, contributing to Long Island's growing underground economy, and thus avoid paying state and federal income taxes on the rental income.

Municipal response to the illegal landlord-tenant relationship has been local accessory apartment laws that register these apartments, which results in proportional increases in property taxes. However this approach has not been widely embraced, since it is the cost of housing and the resulting property tax increases that have driven the illegal tenancy in the first place. Enforcing zoning codes, while legal and vital to the order of neighborhoods only increases the demand for housing.

Long Island regional planners have estimated that close to 90,000 units of workforce housing are needed to provide shelter for the workforce necessary to sustain the Long Island economy. Confirming this are prior Long Island Regional Planning Board estimates, and a 2003 study by the AFL-CIO that placed the need at nearly 83,000 units.

Incomprehensibly, with Long Island losing young people to other regions, there is little focus on why wages paid to young workers have not kept pace with the cost of housing; or on those who are living in illegal accessory apartments even with local code enforcement; or even those who have moved back into their old bedrooms in their parents homes. While no-one will argue with the need for housing for all Long Islanders why, with the regional economy dependent on keeping our workforce here, is the focus narrowly on those people who earn less than 80 percent of the region's median family income and others who are living in substandard or overcrowded housing or in shelters. Greater emphasis, as Suffolk County is doing, should be on those earning 120 percent of the region's median income.

Furthermore, others have argued that community populations have become less dense per square mile between 1980 and 2000, and would use that as a basis for housing needs, which seems unrealistic when a regional view of Long Island's population is that it has grown denser, primarily due to the 5.7 percent population growth since 1980.

Planning should focus on why density has decreased; the root causes of why young people 24 years of age and lower, now 32.9 percent of Long Island's 2000 population, decreased from 40.5 percent in 1980; and why 25-34 year olds have decreased 16 percent from 1980 to 12.9 percent of the 2000 population. These are glaring unanswered questions, with the policy implications having a significant impact on Long Island's future.

The economics of housing is beginning to fray the social and economic fabric of Long Island. Despite current workforce-housing initiatives, there will continue to be a tremendous unmet housing need by workers required to keep the Long Island economy humming. To succeed, any approach must balance the economics, taxes, and cost of home ownership against preservation of Long Island neighborhoods and open space. To date, finding that balance has been elusive.

Immigration: Sustaining a Workforce

Long Island, because of its higher standard of living, and with Suffolk County being the largest agricultural county in the State of New York, the region has become the destination of choice for immigrants, many of which are undocumented. This factor has caused heated debates over national and local immigration policies.

Spirited discussion over immigration policies is not new to the United States, which is odd for a country comprised of immigrants. Each debate is unique to each generation, which is why it is important for federal participation in the current debate over immigration. This is important to localities, because immigration policies, laws, and the authority and resources to enforce them, begin and end with the Federal Government.

There is much disagreement as to how to address today's immigration problem. Any initiative must address two important considerations. The first is recognizing that rounding up for deportation the estimated 11 million undocumented immigrants already here is more difficult and more expensive than the United States debt bulging federal budget can absorb. The other is the cost to many of America's local economies that rely on this inexpensive labor force for delivery of goods and services.

The first notion to overcome is that there is nothing wrong with debating immigration policy. Debate over immigration policies in the United States has been frequent since the birth of the nation, and especially since the 1960's. The Immigration Act of 1965 replaced the national quota system that limited immigration to a designated amount from each country, with a system of graded preferences including workers with needed skills. The Immigration and Nationality Act amendments of 1976 limited the entry of professionals, who usually circumvented this exception by applying under family reunification. Finally, the Immigration Reform and Control Act of 1986 called for immigrants unable to achieve a legal status here to return home.

What was common to all the immigration laws, which other than 1965 restricted immigration, is that they dealt with the concerns of their day, just as the policy alternatives currently under discussion. Complicating the current immigration dilemma is the dynamic created by the economic and trade policies of the North American Hemisphere. Both the Canadian and North American Free Trade Agreements have made it easier to trade among nations by removing tariffs and loosening border restrictions, with the comparatively strong United States economy and job market attracting a flow of labor through a porous Mexican border.

What is inescapable is that as baby boomers age and retire, new workers must be found to continue America's economic growth and provide taxes to fund the very government programs that the retirees will rely on. This is especially true for Long Island where retiring baby boomers occupy a significant portion of the population. Only through legal integration into the American society and economy will assimilation for those seeking citizenship begin, and a new workforce developed to sustain both the national and regional economies.

For Long Island to grow, a balance must be achieved between the new immigrants to Long Island and existing residents. To do less will relegate the region to chasing dreams beyond its capability to achieve. The result is that no one will benefit.

Sustaining Household Budgets: Reliable and Reasonable Energy Costs

Energy costs have been one of the most important issues confronting Long Island. It is an issue that just won't go away. From the for-profit Long Island Lighting Company (LILCO) to the current government-owned Long Island Lighting Company (LIPA), the delivery of energy to Long Islanders is a debate that just won't die.

LILCO was a reviled public utility that created an increasing spiral of rate increases to cover costs resulting from its ill-fated strategy of creating a nuclear energy facility. The result was over $6 billion in debt that had to be configured into the rate base. A state initiative to control these costs resulted in the publicly owned LIPA, which purchased the electricity delivery grid from LILCO. This resulted in immediate lower electric rates merely because of LIPA's not-for-profit status that saved the utility from paying stockholders dividends and federal and state corporate taxes. However, missing an opportunity for further rate reductions was that there were never any significant LIPA operational efficiencies resulting in ratepayer savings. And with the cost of oil increasing to current levels, the LIPA surcharges on Long Islander's electric bills have wiped out the original ratepayer savings resulting from the formation of LIPA. Absorbing these rate increases have been regional household and business budgets.

Ironically, just when you thought that Long Island's energy picture was resolved, even though that resolution brought rate increases, along comes the British industrial giant National Grid, which is in the process of acquiring KeySpan Energy, the public utility that has managed the LIPA electrical delivery system since LIPA's formation. This within a short period after KeySpan and LIPA agreed in November 2005 to terms of a new management contract, with KeySpan continuing to operate and maintain LIPA's transmission and distribution system.

If the sale of KeySpan goes through, as seems to be the case, it will be the first time that Long Island's energy will be controlled by off Long Island management. LIPA will remain, as will a local labor force. However any profit decisions will be made somewhere else, quite possibly in England, a long distance from the pain from workforce reductions and from the higher rates paid by every Long Island business and household. However, the fact that LIPA has a nontransferable management agreement with KeySpan, should KeySpan be sold LIPA may be able to exert some leverage, and be able to extract concessions from National Grid, such as short-term reasonable energy rates and labor force and service delivery protections.

Labor force and service stability cannot be minimized since National Grid is a for-profit company that has projected a rate of return on the $42 per share buy-out cost of KeySpan, profits that will have to be extracted from the operations, and the workforce, in short order. Long Islanders are already griping about the length of time for a service call.

It is also delusional to believe that Long Island energy costs will go anywhere but up in the future, since the price of oil will never go back to the levels in the mid 1990's when LIPA fuel surcharges did not exist. The best Long Island can hope for is a freeze of all rates for a period of time, but that will be short lived, since there is nearly $7 billion of LIPA debt to service, which will be a factor in future energy rates. There is also the need to repower some of LIPA's existing power plants, with the result of generating cleaner and more efficient energy production. The burning question is who will bear the estimated $1 billion repowering cost. Clearly the ratepayer will be a factor here since it is unrealistic to think National Grid stockholders will pay any of the repowering costs.

As usual, Long Island's future economic competitive business advantage, and sustainable household discretionary income are tied to energy costs.

The Regional Tax Base: Financing Municipal Services and School Districts

American tax policy has always been based upon a progressive taxing system where everyone pays his or her fare share. This philosophy has wealthier taxpayers shoulder a greater burden than those who are struggling to survive.

Property taxes, which have long financed Long Island school districts and municipal government, were once thought of as progressive. That is, if one can afford a more expensive house then one should be able to afford the taxes on that home. However this relationship has become skewed with assessed valuations increasing to reflect current market conditions, without regard to the ability of the homeowner's wages rising at the same levels to pay for the increasing tax burden. The result has been rising tax levies to pay for growing school, town and local budgets. Long Island's once progressive system of taxation has become regressive, with taxes now consuming a larger part of a family's budget, something not intended when the property tax system was implemented.

The time has come to seriously begin considering replacing the regressive property tax system with a more progressive and equitable taxing structure to finance school districts and local government. There may never be a more opportune moment, as local government and civic leaders are searching for answers on how to keep more young people in the Nassau/Suffolk region. All agree that the region's economic future is dependent on making Long Island affordable for young workers, necessary to replace the larger workforce demographic group of retiring baby boomers.

If wrong decisions are made, the result will be a diminishing tax base and erosion of the local economy. The cause will be an inequitable burden of a greater proportion of school and local taxes normally paid for by the retiring members of the regional workforce now being shifted to the smaller demographic group of younger workers. These young workers will be required to pay taxes at a greater proportion of their after-tax income, replacing the burden once borne by the retiring baby boomers.

This takes on greater importance given current demographic changes to the Long Island population and the impact that the global economy has had on Long Island's economic sectors. During the past decade more immigrants have called Long Island home at the same time that the global economy has placed a greater demand for workers with technology skills. These higher paying technology jobs require a greater degree of intellectual capability and educational attainment that new immigrants do not have, and have replaced the blue-collar sustainable jobs that immigrants once could fill. The result has been a growing divide in Long Island's employment base comprised of those making more, and those making less. Those making more usually possess a higher degree of educational attainment, enabling them to access the higher paying jobs created by the Long Island economy. Those making less usually have a lower level of educational attainment and thus only able to access the lower paying service and wholesale and retail jobs.

For the region, this situation is becoming one of equity for Long Island's newest neighbors. If they can afford to rent housing, they tend to live in traditionally poorer communities without industrial and commercial property tax bases where the amount spent per student is less. If they can afford to buy a house, it is often in the property tax starved school districts where housing costs are lower, but where property taxes as a percentage of housing costs are disproportionably higher, removing vital after tax income from the local economy. Furthermore, the higher property taxes as a percentage of after tax income limits any chance for these home owners of accumulating the capital necessary in a Long Island society where the cost of living makes upward socio-economic mobility difficult.

With all these factors taken into consideration, it is obvious that the system by which the region funds its school districts and local government is broken and needs fixing. Recent increases in school budgets, while wages continue to stagnate, suggest that the local tax base is nearing a breaking point. One alternative worth investigating is a bifurcated system that would retain the property tax on commercial properties for schools and local government, while replacing the residential school and local property tax with a modest income tax to be paid for by homeowners (including co-ops and condos) and renters of real property.

A regional income tax would broaden the tax base to include the 964,000 Long Islanders who file state income tax returns with taxable income, thereby adding over 230,000 taxpayers to a local school tax base, exceeding the nearly 734,000 owner occupied homeowners paying property taxes. Progressiveness would be returned to Long Island's base because not taxed under this system would be the over 281,000 Long Islanders filing state returns without any tax liability.

While property taxes are based on a fair market value system of assessment, rising with market value usually not accompanied by cash to pay the property tax, a modest income tax will be imposed on the approximately $776 billion in New York State adjusted gross income currently earned by Long Islanders.

Changing the system that funds school budgets and local governments equalizes the burden on education on a broader and fairer tax base, allows for a more mobile society, and reduces crushing property taxes from becoming the overwhelming factor to where one lives. Properly conceived, the regional income tax will alleviate the inequities in achieving these goals.

Race: Institutional Racism, Entrepreneurship, Obstacles To Wealth Accumulation

What has become apparent since the end of World War II is that racist segregation on Long Island is no longer a secret, and fair housing, or lack thereof, has become part of the institutional racism on Long Island. Institutional racism in the Long Island region is all around, and when you think about it, we have all seen it. According to local groups, institutional racism is comprised of policies, structures and behaviors that create or encourage segregation and inequality in every aspect of our daily living. Just think about how racism impacts economics, education, employability, and wealth accumulation for Long Islanders of color, and how ending institutional racial inequity can enhance the Long Island economy. The analysis of the four communities presented is a stark realization of this.

What better illustration of that inequity is there than the wealth accumulation that is associated with the current value of Long Island homes, as compared to how much was paid for them? What's inequitable is not the value of the investment or the amount of the profit, it's the ability of everyone in this region, if able, to access these properties. But this is not a new problem.

The practice of excluding people of color from purchasing homes where they can afford has been around for years, and accelerated, as discussed, with the development of Levittown, America's first suburb. Levittown was a place where veterans returning home after serving in the armed forces during World War II could find a place to live that was affordable and had a quality of life to raise a family. However, as history has shown, the process of securing a Levittown home was not favorable to all veterans, with white veterans receiving preference over blacks.

The result was that black Americans, if they found housing on Long Island, were concentrated in segregated communities such as Gordon Heights, North Amityville, and Roosevelt, while others found housing in the segregated communities of the region's urban centers such as New York. Irwin Quintyne represented that.

Despite the Civil Rights and Fair Housing Acts passed during the 1960's, the practice of housing discrimination continued well into the 1970's. In particular, black Americans living in New York City, and wishing to move to Long Island and the promise of Levittown, were directed by some realtors to Long Island's existing segregated communities such as North Amityville. What other explanation is there for why in 1970 only five percent of the Suffolk County population was black as compared to 66 percent of North Amityville. By 1990 blacks in Suffolk County grew slightly to six percent of the population, as compared to 78 percent in North Amityville. As we begin this new millennium, the situation has not improved. The question is what then does the Long Island region need to do?

One answer is in a recent effort by Erase Racism, a Syosset advocacy group. What Erase Racism is trying to accomplish is to create a local administrative system to give people who feel they have not been given fair housing opportunities the access to the system to provide them with due process in the pursuit of housing that other Long Islanders have been able to achieve. Both Nassau and Suffolk County have embraced the concept in differing degrees. Nassau County has established a local law that establishes a local process to deal with fair housing inequities. Suffolk County wants New York State to become the enforcement agency. What is important is that both counties begin the process of providing equal housing opportunities to all. Housing integration benefits all of Long Island, and is the most important asset that families have toward wealth accumulation.

Why all Long Islanders should be concerned is that as we confront the socio-economic challenges demanded by the global economy, the fastest way to expand our regional economy is to create equal opportunities for all. Increasing the wealth of those Long Islanders who have not participated in past growth is much less costly, and produces a better economic return of regional investment than by attracting economic growth from outside the region.

One policy initiative that can grow Long Island economic activity from within is to encourage minority entrepreneurship. The presented analysis reveals that there are untapped minority entrepreneurs in each of the nine presented communities, which indicates that there is growth potential in Suffolk County's entrepreneurial class, each representing a potential business. Experience indicates that many entrepreneurs begin by operating out of a home or garage. Providing incentives that not only encourage cultivation of Suffolk County minority entrepreneurs, but also concentrates their economic activity in their respective community business district, will provide an important economic spark that can contribute to revitalizing their individual downtowns. As previously noted, by attracting entrepreneurs to underserved central business districts, storefronts will become occupied; vacant land built upon, and dilapidated buildings rehabilitated. Customer and pedestrian traffic increases, and new economic activity is generated. As a critical mass of economic activity evolves, the downtown eventually becomes stronger than its individual parts. One way to accomplish this is with the creation of business and technology incubators in minority community business districts.

One such effort is in North Amityville, where the North Amityville Community Economic Council is sponsoring a 20,000 square foot business incubator in the final phase of revitalizing the community. Not coincidentally, the driving forces in this effort are the late Irwin Quintyne, Rosemarie Dearing and Lenny Canton, the same community leaders whose descriptions of their community are told in the opening pages of this book. Suffolk County has also developed a business incubator initiative where capital dollars and technical assistance is being provided to community based organizations wishing to encourage entrepreneurs by establish business incubators in their communities.

There is a lesson to be learned in this debate on where Long Island is heading as we become more sociologically and economically diverse. Unless attitudes change, and an atmosphere created where every Long Islander, with equal means, can open their own business and have access to housing of their choice, we are holding back the growth of the Long Island economy.

Land Use and Downtown Revitalization: Preserving Open Space and Farm Land

If there ever was a time that Long Island, and especially the rural east end, was at the crossroads of development and land preservation, that time is upon us. Land use decisions currently under consideration will go a long way towards deciding the future of the east end of Long Island. How it will look, who will live there, and what the traffic patterns will be.

Current zoning codes in the east end towns of Long Island, allowing for development of residential homes on existing farmland, have already wiped out hundreds of acres of farmland while transforming a bucolic tourism destination into a bustling residential community. If liberal development regulations remain as is, the east end's future population, and the Town of Riverhead in particular could triple, requiring increased property taxes to pay for the additional municipal services such as schools, police, water usage, and road maintenance.

With development in Riverhead at the former Naval Base at Calverton expected to commence shortly, and with it traffic and congestion, the east end region should resist the urge to continue approving subdivision requests, and pause to review each's land use policy in the perspective of each other. Current development pressures warrant a fresh look, especially when new planning policies such as Smart Growth are being offered as an alternative to suburban sprawl. By so doing, all the east end towns, Riverhead, Southampton and East Hampton in particular, can find alternatives to their land use policy review.

In particular, a land preservation study considered by the Riverhead Town Board illustrates the problems confronting preserving open space. The study, which suggests restricting development on just 15 percent of each farm parcel is similar to policies under consideration in the neighboring town Southampton which is wrestling with development regulations that would have developers build on only 20 percent of land, leaving the remaining 80 percent as open space. Both would exceed East Hampton Town which currently is the most restrictive in land use by mandating that 70 percent of a farm be left as open space when developed.

Another issue to address is population density as well as land preservation. Allowing homes on 8,000 square feet, equivalent to one-fifth of an acre as Riverhead's study suggests, would change the rural nature of Eastern Long Island. Density allowances providing for building 5 houses per acre when current zoning prohibits no more than one home could result in as many as five times more people and automobiles per acre than is currently allowed. The concern now is to reduce population density on land use as well as to mitigate the increasing automobile traffic. Greater density allowances produce the opposite result. If preserving farmland, controlling population density and limiting traffic are the ultimate goals, as they should be, other options should be explored.

One such option recently unveiled by the Town of Riverhead is a comprehensive downtown revitalization overhaul that includes housing, waterfront development, and new commercial economic activity. This should draw the housing demand to the downtown area, where it can contribute to downtown revitalization efforts. With the Long Island Railroad nearby, the revitalization will encourage pedestrian traffic, and take advantage of the economic activity that can be encouraged from Riverhead's transit-oriented development opportunities.

With downtown revitalization development alternatives available to developers, and new property tax ratables available to towns, open space zoning codes can be tightened, so as to require more open space in each subdivision request.

In the case of the Town of Riverhead, this development alternative is already happening. Yet despite this, residential subdivisions, available water supplies, close proximity to the Long Island Expressway and lower land clearing costs are preferable to developers, because when built upon they yield greater profits. These attributes have created a land rush in Riverhead where a reported 2,300 homes are envisioned for 2,000 acres.

Nonetheless the development clock is ticking in other areas of Riverhead and the other

East End towns, with the final build-out of Long Island expected within the next ten years. If left unchecked, the development boom in the East End of Long Island may destroy the very serenity that attracted the new residents there in the first place.

Seemingly ignored in the land preservation discussion is the financial impact to the family farm. Any decisions Eastern Long Island towns make must address the status of the family farm and insure that farmers receive fair compensation for the loss of any value to their land caused by future land use decisions. If zoning changes ultimately require that residential homes require five acres instead of two, land has less competitive value to a developer. Farmers should not have to bear that burden alone. Enough resources could be generated through a combination of funding from Suffolk County's Open Space Program, town bonding, and the East End real property transfer tax. These future revenues should be dedicated to repaying a special revenue bond to accelerate land purchases.

Municipalities with multi sector economies must decide what to build their economy around and where to invest their resources. For the East End of Long Island it's tourism, farming, fishing, retail, and downtown revitalization. Preserving farmland from development, and insuring that farmers are compensated for not developing their land makes sense.

If it's solely tourism, then barring new golf courses in the agricultural zones makes no sense. The options are many, but doing nothing should not be one of them. Unless coordinated and stricter land use policies are adopted and coordinated region wide, the open spaces once enjoyed by many may not be around for future generations of Long Islanders.

Transportation: Commercial Traffic and Road Capacity

Visionary planner Robert Moses' view of what Long Island should look like resulted in the current road network that brought from the west the people and materials that would change Long Island's landscape forever. The Long Island of Robert Moses became a "bedroom" community, where most Long Islanders came home to sleep after working in New York City.

Moses saw how an interlocking network of roads would lead to the expansion and economic development of Long Island. How Long Island supports the changing needs of today's transportation infrastructure will go a long way in determining what the region's future economy will look like.

However, contemporary Long Island is much different from what Moses encountered. Contemporary Long Island has become a self-sustaining economic entity where most who work here live here, with a lesser percentage commuting to jobs in New York City. This changing work pattern has resulted in increased regional economic activity, greater traffic flow to support that activity, and increasing demands for a transportation infrastructure capable of sustaining that heightened level of transportation originated congestion and economic activity.

With Long Island's appetite for transportation capacity growing with each passing day, and with the Long Island Expressway's HOV lane completed, there are few road improvements left to relieve regional traffic congestion. Furthermore, the time necessary to implement transportation projects that relieve congestion can take almost eight years, with much of that time spent on research, evaluation, planning, design and public vetting.

There is an alternative to building more road capacity. It is by removing trucks from regional roads by shipping goods and trailers off Long Island by rail. The benefits are many. The first is the removal of as many as possible of the 53-foot tractor and trailers from Long Island's commercial roadways, since each is estimated to be the equivalent to removing 7 automobiles from the roadways. The second is that with nearly 66 percent of the New York City regional freight traveling on the I-95 corridor, are the potential financial savings for truckers who now have to pay a daily premium for the extra time necessary to transverse Long Island's congested roadways, and who then have to travel north to Newburgh to find a suitable roadway west. The third is the lessening of pollution caused by idling trucks as they try to move their products West.

The good news is that the New York State Department of Transportation planning process has caught up with Long Island's need. The NYSDOT has a coordinated series of projects, which when completed, can remove as many as 1,000 trucks daily from the LIE. They are the proposed Long Island Rail-Truck Inter-Modal Facility on the Pilgrim State property in Brentwood that will transfer the trailers from the tractors to flatbed railcars; a third rail for the Long Island Railroad to accommodate the increased flatbed freight and commuter traffic; and a Cross-Harbor Tunnel connecting Brooklyn to New Jersey. When completed, Long Island truckers will be able to transfer their trailers to flatbed rail cars and have that flatbed rail car travel on available LIRR rail capacity through the cross-harbor tunnel where tractors will meet them in New Jersey for the trip west.

For Long Island these improvements make sense. The current LIRR tracks are nearing capacity in handling the region's robust passenger service and can't accommodate the additional freight service. There is also a tremendous imbalance between the methods of moving freight West. New York State Department of Transportation data estimates that over 80 percent of regional freight move by truck, as compared to less than 1 percent moving by rail. This rail use rate, the lowest in the United States, is due to freight tunnel height restrictions unable to accommodate double stack capacity for rail East of the Hudson River, including trailers on flatbed railcars.

For Long Island the choice is simple. Either choke on regional economic growth, or develop transit-oriented transportation projects designed to move freight off regional roadways to the railroad.

Global Long Island: Final Thoughts

"Are you better off today than you were four years ago?" Ronald Reagan asked that of American voters in 1980, who responded by sending incumbent President Jimmy Carter home to Georgia and Reagan to the White House.

While twenty-six years may not be a long time, Reagan's question remains as relevant today, when comparing the 1980 economic climate of the United States to 2006. In 1980 wages earned by Americans were diluted by runaway inflation, stagflation and double-digit interest rates. Today, interest rates have increased from their record low levels, and there is concern for inflation from higher interest rates, and energy costs. As in 1980 economic stress confronting contemporary American households remain, despite being driven by different factors than 20 years ago. Today global economic pressures strongly influence the regional economy.

The global economy in 1980 was very different than it is today. In 1980 the United States was a producing nation, with the domestic balance of trade having a modest trade deficit of $19.6 billion, with imports exceeding exports. Comprising that deficit, which was nine percent of imports, was a modest surplus in manufacturing and agricultural exports, offset primarily by a significant deficit in imported oil and natural gas. Today, the United States has become a purchasing nation, with an exploding trade deficit with imports significantly exceeding exports. Manufacturing imports significantly exceed exports with the agricultural surplus falling and the imported oil and natural gas trade deficit increasing.

So the question is how Long Islanders will react to the changing world economy, which since 1990 has forced Long Island to survive several recessions, rising interest rates, higher taxes, increases in the cost of living, a changing regional job market, fickle foreign markets, stagnating wages, and the role that technology has played in these changes.

As has been said often, and worth repeating, is that between 1980 and 2000 Long Island experienced the de-industrialization of its manufacturing base, which continues to shrink, caused in part by the contraction of the region's defense industry. Where as Long Island once had prime military contractors such as Fairchild-Republic, Eaton, Sperry, Hazeltine, and Grumman Corp., today it has none. This contraction has led to manufacturing workforce reductions, which continue today, impacting much of the regions less skilled and less educated workers. At the same time, influenced largely by the globalization of economic events, the demand for more skilled and more educated workers has been growing in Long Island's high technology industries, and in the growing financial and banking sector. Sadly, latest regional job statistics have been disappointing and suggest inconsistent and slow job growth.

There are other economic storm clouds to consider. The workforce that Long Island prides itself with and depends upon for continuance of its economic growth is shrinking. The regional workforce, just over 50 percent of the 1990 population has now fallen to 48 percent of the 2000 Long Island population. The cause for the decrease seems to be Long Island's newest residents, who comprised all of Long Island's population growth since 1990. These new Long Islanders may have difficulties entering the workforce because their lower level of education attainment results in skills that limits their ability to access the technological and critical thinking jobs being created on Long Island and required of the global economy. Of concern is that a shrinking of the qualified and available workforce may lead to corporate relocations off Long Island and a contraction of the regional economy.

Also worrisome is that Long Island's educated workforce may be ebbing, taking with it the region's capacity to earn higher wages. While college enrollments have decreased since 1990, growth rates in Elementary/High School are more than twice the rate of preliminary school enrollments. While college education doesn't guarantee a higher paying job, former Labor Secretary Robert Reich observed that without that education a higher paying job is out of reach. What is alarming is that the combination of a shrinking workforce and a workforce with fewer higher paid workers will lead to reduced consumer spending. The result will be a contraction of retail and wholesale jobs and the ripple effect of these job losses further percolating through the regional economy costing more job losses. Further damage will be a reduction in the sales tax collections that are so important in financing regional government.

So the mystery of what Long Island is to become is yet before us. To be sure, the requirements to succeed in the global economy are much more complex than what was required for success in the economy and society during the heady days after the end of World War II, when returning veterans found their way here and built America's first suburb. How Long Island succeeds, and what it will look like, will be very dependent on how Long Islanders adapt to the constant changes in the global economy; how we accept our newest residents; and how we understand the economic potential of communities of color and the importance of economic equality and opportunity.

BIBLIOGRAPHY

North Amityville

Canton, Lenny. Personal interview. 18 May 2001. 27 August 2006.

Dearing, Rosemarie. Personal interview. 18 May 2001. 27 August 2006.

First Precinct, Suffolk County, New York Police Department. *North Amityville Weed and Seed Presentation.* South Oaks Chapel Auditorium. 11 September 1998.

Moritsugu, Ken. "Driving Out Drugs-Town OKs Renewal Plan in N. Amityville." *Newsday.* 21 April 1994.

New York State Data Center, Department of Economic Development. *1990 Census of Population and Housing - Summary Tape File 3 - Selected Characteristics.* April, 1992

New York State Labor Department of Labor. *Occupational Outlook, Long Island Region. Long Island Labor Market Information.*Online. Internet, 11 June 2001. Available http://www.wdsny.org/longisle/top.htm

Quintyne, Irwin. Personal interview. 18 May 2001.

Reich, Robert B. *The Works of Nations.* New York: Vintage Books, 1992.

Riley Lt., Edward. "Weed and Seed" Police commander, First Precinct, Suffolk County, Town of Babylon. Personal interview. 16 November 1998.

Sassen, Saskia. *The Global City: New York, London, Tokyo.* Princeton: Princeton University Press, 1991.

Tilak, Jandhyala B.G. *Education and Its Relation to Economic Growth, Poverty, and Income Distribution.* Washington: The World Bank, May 1990.

United States. President's Council on Sustainable Development. *A New Consensus for Prosperity, Opportunity and a Healthy Environment for the Future.* Washington, D.C. Feburary 1996.

United States. Bureau of the Census. 1970 Census of Population and Housing. *New York, N.Y. Standard Metropolitan Statistical Area (Parts 1,2,3).* Washington, GPO, May 1972. Table P-1: General Characteristics of the Population: 1970 Table P-2: Social Characteristics of the Population: 1970 Table P-3: Labor Force Characteristics of the Population: 1970

Table P-4: Income Characteristics of the Population: 1970
Table H-1: Occupancy, Utilization and Financial Characteristics of Housing Units

United States. Bureau of the Census. 1990 Census of Population and Housing. *Summary Social, Economic, and Housing Characteristics of New York*. Washington: GPO, April 1992.
Table 3: Education and Veteran Status
Table 15: Homeowner and Renter Characteristics: 1990

United States. Bureau of the Census. 1990 Census of Population and Housing. *Population and Housing Characteristics for Census Tracts and Block Numbering Areas for New York-Northern New Jersey*. Washington: GPO, July 1993.
Table 1:   General Characteristics of Persons
Table 15:   Land Area and Population Density
Table 17:   Social Characteristics of Persons
Table 18:   Labor Force and Disability Characteristics of Persons
Table 22:   Social and Labor Force Characteristics of Black Person
Table 23:   Occupation, Income in 1989, and Poverty Status in 1989 of Black Persons: 1990.

United States. Bureau of the Census. 1990 Census of the Population. *Social and Economic Characteristics of New York*. Washington: GPO, September 1993.
Table 1:   General Characteristics of Persons
Table 57:   Household and Family Characteristic by Race
Table 61:   Age and Sex by Race and Hispanic Origin: 1990
Table 148:   Income in 1989,Households,Families and Person: 1990
Table 152:   Education, Ability to Speak English: 1990
Table 154:   Labor Force Characteristics by Race and Hispanic Orig
Table 156:   Occupation of Employed Person by Race/Hispanic Orig

Wilson, William Julius. *When Work Disappears, The World of the New Urban Poor*. New York: Alfred A. Knopf, 1997.

Huntington Station

Huntington Town Board. *General Neighborhood Renewal Plan, Huntington Station Area*. Huntington, New York. November, 1962.

New York State Data Center, Department of Economic Development. *1990 Census of Population and Housing - Summary Tape File 3 - Selected Characteristics*. April, 1992.

Office of Urban Renewal, Town of Huntington. *Facts About LIFT Project No. 1*. Huntington, New York, 1966.

Sforza, Alfred V. *Portrait of A Small Town.* New York: Maple Hill Press, 1996.

The Town of Huntington Planning Department. *Report on The Huntington Station Moratorium Area.* Huntington, New York. 5 August 2003.

Thompson, Dolores. Personal Interview. 23 May 2006.

United States. Bureau of the Census. *1990 Census, Population of Housing Summary Tape File 1 and 3* (STF 1 and 3). Online. Internet, 15 June 2003. Available, http://Factfinder.census.gov/home/en/datanotes.
    Table DP-1: General Population and Housing Characteristics: 1990.
    Table DP-2: Social Characteristics: 1990.
    Table DP-3: Labor Force Status and Employment Characteristics: 1990
    Table DP-4: Income and Poverty Status in 1989: 1990.

United States. Bureau of the Census. *Census 2000 Summary File 1* (SF-1). Online. Internet, 15 June 2003. Available, http://Factfinder.census.gov/bf.
    Table DP-1: Profile of General Demographic Characteristics: 2000.

Roosevelt

Guilty, Andreaus. Personal interview. 31 May 2006.

New York State Data Center, Department of Economic Development. *1990 Census of Population and Housing - Summary Tape File 3 - Selected Characteristics.* April, 1992.

New York State Department of Labor. *Occupational Outlook, Long Island Region. Long Island Labor Market Information.* Online. Internet, 11 June 2001. Available, http://www.wdsny.org/longisle/top.htm.

Tilak, Jandhyala G.G. *Education and Its Relation to Economic Growth, Poverty, and Income Distribution.* Washington: The World Bank, May 1990.

United States. Bureau of the Census. *1990 Census, Population of Housing Summary Tape File 1 and 3* (STF 1 and 3). Online. Internet, 21 June 2002. Available, http://Factfinder.census.gov/home/en/datanotes.
    Table DP-1: General Population and Housing Characteristics: 1990.
    Table DP-2: Social Characteristics: 1990.
    Table DP-3: Labor Force Status and Employment Characteristics: 1990
    Table DP-4: Income and Poverty Status in 1989: 1990.

United States. Bureau of the Census. *Census 2000 Summary File 1* (SF-1). Online. Internet, 22 June 2002. Available, http://Factfinder.census.gov/bf.
    Table DP-1: Profile of General Demographic Characteristics: 2000.

Table DP-2: Profile of Selected Social Characteristics: 2000.
Table DP-3: Profile of Selected Economic Characteristics: 2000.
Table DP-2: Profile of Selected Social Characteristics: 2000.
Table DP-3: Profile of Selected Economic Characteristics: 2000.

Port Washington

Infoshare.org.-Source: Bureau of the Census, U.S. Department of Commerce; Region, New York State; Zip Code 11050, Port Washington. On Line 21 February 2005.

United States. Bureau of the Census. *1990 Census, Population of Housing Summary Tape File 1 and 3* (STF 1 and 3). Online. Internet, 21 June 2002. Available, http://Factfinder.census.gov/home/en/datanotes.
    Table DP-1: General Population and Housing Characteristics: 1990.
    Table DP-2: Social Characteristics: 1990.
    Table DP-3: Labor Force Status and Employment Characteristics: 1990
    Table DP-4: Income and Poverty Status in 1989: 1990.

United States. Bureau of the Census. *Census 2000 Summary File 1* (SF-1). Online. Internet, 22 June 2002. Available, http://Factfinder.census.gov/bf.
    Table DP-1: Profile of General Demographic Characteristics: 2000.
    Table DP-2: Profile of Selected Social Characteristics: 2000.
    Table DP-3: Profile of Selected Economic Characteristics: 2000.

Suffolk County Minority Entrepreneurship

United States. Bureau of the Census. *2000 Census, Sex By Industry By Class of Worker For The Employed Civilian Population 16 Years and Over (65)*. Data Set: Census 2000 Summary File 4. Online. Internet, 30 May 2005. Available http://factfinder.census.gov/home/en/datanotes/expsf4.htm.

Research Assistant: Bradley R. Cantor, MS, Urban Planning